RELEASED

ACADEMIC POWER IN ITALY

ACADEMIC POWER
IN ITALY

Bureaucracy and Oligarchy in
a National University System

BURTON R. CLARK

ST. JOSEPH'S UNIVERSITY
LB2341.8.I8C55   STX
Academic power in Italy :

3 9353 00072 4359

178852

LB
2341.8
·I8
C55

THE UNIVERSITY OF CHICAGO PRESS
Chicago and London

BURTON R. CLARK is professor of sociology and chairman of the Program of Comparative and Historical Studies of Higher Education at Yale University. He is the author of *Adult Education in Transition*, *The Distinctive College*, and *The Open Door College*.

THE UNIVERSITY OF CHICAGO PRESS, CHICAGO 60637
THE UNIVERSITY OF CHICAGO PRESS, LTD., LONDON
© 1977 by The University of Chicago
All rights reserved. Published 1977
Printed in the United States of America
81 80 79 78 77   987654321

LIBRARY OF CONGRESS CATALOGING IN PUBLICATION DATA

Clark, Burton R
  Academic power in Italy.

  Bibliography: p.
  Includes index.
  1. Universities and colleges—Italy—Administration.
I. Title.
LB2341.8.I8C55   378.45   77-4010
ISBN 0-226-10847-3

To Adele

CONTENTS

ACKNOWLEDGMENTS

It is not possible, or even considerate, to attempt to list the persons in Italy who responded to my intrusions in the face of hectic daily schedules that are part of Italian academic life. I was warned before going to Italy that I would face broken appointments. There were none. It only took some adjustment of American punctuality to otherwise smooth the way. For facilitating my initial contacts, I am indebted to Joseph La Palombara, Yale University, and Alberto Spreafico, an Italian political scientist, who was at the time secretary of a joint American-Italian committee working on the improvement of social science in Italy. For daily assistance in gaining access to documents, carrying out interviews, and observing Italian academic life, I wish to thank, as successive research assistants, Anna Perrotta, Francesco De-Domenico, Giovanna Pennachi, and Anna Giambartolomei, all of Rome. During the writing of this report, between 1972 and 1975, I was able to draw on a small group of Italian friends knowledgeable about the Italian university system for criticism of drafts: Alessandro Cavalli, Alberto Martinelli, and Guido Martinotti, in Milan; Giampaolo Bonani, Sergio Bruno, Giuseppe DeRita, and Francesco D'Onofrio, in Rome; and Pier Paolo Giglioli, in Bologna, who generously shared with me the interpretations and data of his dissertation and book (in progress) on the Italian academic man. I also profited from participation in a Rome seminar on Italian higher education organized by James Perkins, chairman, International Council for Educational Development, in the summer of 1972, and from the report of that seminar, referred to later, prepared by Barbara Burn. None of the above is responsible for the interpretations of the Italian system presented in this study.

The fieldwork underlying this study began in the summer of 1967 and was carried out mainly while I was on sabbatical leave in 1968-69. I returned to Italy in 1972, 1973, and 1974 on short visits that seasoned my understanding of Italian education and society. The trips were made possible through the support of two organizations: Yale University, which granted me a Senior Faculty Fellowship for the first leave and aided a second period of reflection during 1972-73; and the National Science Foundation which, through two successive research grants, supported my own efforts in Italy between 1968 and 1973 as well as the allied research of younger colleagues and graduate students in other countries. I am most grateful to the university and the foundation for patient and trusting aid. A growing awareness on my part of the problems of research support in other countries has enlarged my appreciation for the private and public agencies in this country that fund a scholar to do as he pleases.

Since 1973, the support of my effort to engage in comparative analysis of national academic control has been assumed by the National Institute of Education, the Lilly Endowment, and the Institution for Social and Policy Studies (ISPS) at Yale. This support has made possible the initiation of a Program of Historical and Comparative Studies of Higher Education within the Yale ISPS, which in turn, beginning in 1973-74, has been able to support pre- and postdoctoral fellows and visiting scholars in a concentrated effort to help turn the comparative and historical study of higher education into a sustained scholarly enterprise worthy of such a major social institution. My study of the Italian system has benefited from the seminars of this program and the research it has supported. The next best thing to being an expert on every country is to assemble experts with whom one can interact intensively.

Margaret Anbar, Mary Hyson, Rotha Lane, Mary Markiza, and Joleen Scott, secretaries at Yale, and Linda Charest and Frances O'Dell of Editorial Associates, typed the several versions of the manuscript. Barbara Baird Ryan, director of Editorial Associates, supervised the preparation of the two last drafts, and I am particularly indebted to her for substantive revisions as well as editing of the final copy. I wish especially to thank my wife, Adele Clark, for assistance in many ways.

A note on sources: for an English-language work, I have, wherever possible in references, used documents that have appeared in English over Italian ones, even when the English publications were clearly derivative. I hope by this approach to encourage further reading on the topic, as well as to allow readers greater opportunity to check what is said against other sources. Italian sources other than basic government documents and statistical reports have been used sparingly. There is a shortage of relevant literature in Italy, more than in France or Germany, but I hope that I have used what there is in a way that gives credit to the few Italian scholars who have concentrated their attention on the Italian university system.

Having long held that nothing was to be learned by us from the foreigners, we are at last beginning to see, that on a matter like the institution of schools, for instance, much light is thrown by a comparative study of their institution among other civilized states and nations. To treat this comparative study with proper respect, not to wrest it to the requirements of our inclinations or prejudices, but to try simply and seriously to find what it teaches us, is perhaps the lesson which we have most need to inculcate upon ourselves at present.

Matthew Arnold
Schools and Universities on the Continent

INTRODUCTION

This study seeks the realities of academic power in the higher education of an entire nation. Why Italy? For one reason, it has operated a unified national system of universities, making its educational structure the opposite of the American one. For a researcher schooled in the dispersed educational control exercised by fifty states and a private sector, analysis of a centralized system promised to shed light on the far side of basic phenomena of control, defining much of the range over which concepts and categories would have to stretch in cross-national comparison of academic organization. Then, too, in its unitary approach the Italian system is close to the way that most nations around the world have organized and will be organizing higher learning. To develop a comparative understanding of control and influence in educational systems, one must know about national administration, since the nation-state is *the* modern sponsor. Not even the United States, the model of market conditions in higher education, has been immune to the temptation of nationally administered order. On this crucial feature, a nation such as Italy, which has only recently become an advanced industrial society, might also speak to the future experience of developing societies as well as reveal some characteristics shared with such advanced neighbors as France and Germany.

Italy is also intriguing because it has international standing as a case of opaque educational structure. Officials and researchers, in and out of international agencies, who were attempting in the 1960s to gather data and make judgments on national systems of education and research, often found that they knew little about the inner workings of Italian education and reported difficulty in making sense of what the Italians were doing. "Inept bureaucracy" was one of the kinder labels applied. Official reporting from Italy to international councils seemed weak and undependable, resulting in knowledge on even basic facts that was not on a par with that available on the countries of northern Europe. Information often came slowly or not at all, raising suspicion of official bungling and protection of national pride against invidious comparison. Despite the unitary framework, it was not clear whether anyone was in charge and, if so, who. Therefore, Swedes, Englishmen, and others of the North, including Americans, have had great latitude to speculate on the role of hidden hands, black funds, and other secretive ways purportedly buried deep in Italian and Mediterranean character. Here was ideal research territory for a sociologist committed to unearthing latent patterns in national webs of administration as a way of clarifying what otherwise would remain dim to the eye and remote to the touch of reform. To speak to the international view of Italian disorder became an additional challenge.

The early days in the field confirmed that anyone attempting to penetrate the Italian university system would face a curious setting. At first glance, much was on the surface, laid bare in formal rule. On a second glance, practice was heavily shielded in unspoken and confidential ways. And where was power to be observed? Knowledgeable professors sent the researcher to the central agencies in Rome to walk the bleak corridors and knock on the doors of officials. There, equally knowledgeable Italians turned the visitor around and pointed the way back to the offices of the professors. The crossroads of decision were confusing, so shaded that most participants were unsure from day to day what was going on and where to go to find out. Thus there seemed some point to the stereotype of the system as veritable chaos. But then perhaps other large national systems of higher education present the same appearance to investigators who are interested in moving beyond descriptive statistics to the problem of who governs. Our purpose became that of penetrating the Italian system at least to the point of a first approximation of academic power, interpreting its nature in terms that might be useful in other countries and in the comparison of countries.

For this task, the cupboard of ideas and concepts was almost bare, largely limited to broad views of systems of higher education as centralized or decentralized, unitary or federal, competitive or uniformly administered, with the possibility that the broad view, if it did not misplace power, obscured more than it revealed. Our approach was microstructural: to go to the specific settings in which academics work and there determine what they were impelled to do and constrained from doing by the positions they occupied. What were the role mandates of senior professors, junior staff, campus administrators, and central officials? Who had discretion and who did not, and in what policies? Where was power located in the structure, how was it effected, and whose interests were served? To focus on position and power in this fashion is to move inside the large-scale organization of academic life in a way that steers between the uniqueness of individual action and the global characterization of a formal system that leaves unanswered the questions of who does what to whom and why. The effort is to marry political analysis to organizational analysis in the study of academic systems.

This approach avoids easy explanation that jumps quickly to national character, collective mentality, and other broad features of general culture that are supposed to hang in the air of a whole country—and similarly for the easily posited dominance of the church, big business, or ruling political elite. A disciplined approach that begins inside the organized setting of a main social activity is particularly needed for Italy, a country so stereotyped from afar and by its own writers addressing a foreign audience in terms of traditional amoralism, the Mafia-based exercise of power, church control, fumbling political attempts, and inept bureaucratic work. Some of these characteristics may be appropriate, but they are not the place to begin. Rather we need to seek the causes of behavior in the immediate structure that determines whose interests are there expressed and how. Then we can move outward to successively larger structures of causation. Thus the injunction in the explanation of academic power is always to begin with the academic structure itself and then turn to the next larger framework, the administrative structure of government. Beyond that lie the top councils of government, the legislature, and external organized sectors, such as industry and the professions, that may be connected systematically to the specific structure under study. But we need to step out to the wider rings of explanation only as we detect specific connections between the inner and the outer, the bridges over which influence flows. If error must be made, our form of determinism will err by ascribing too much to inside features. But this is a useful and necessary corrective to explanations that underestimate the role of the complex organization as the tool of modern social action. The nature of those tools, whether the British Treasury, the United States Forest Service, the French planning bureau, or the Italian ministry of education, and how they shape behavior, cannot be deduced from studies of other interesting sectors of the same society. If we must worry about larger causation, then the first turn should be to the historical origin and development of the organizations in question. In highly differentiated modern society, bureaus are institutions with something of a historically derived life of their own.

The pages that follow first set forth the crucial historical characteristics of the Italian universities, note the strong forces of fragmentation inherent in this set of institutions, and pose the problem of the making of a "system" (Chapter 1). The analysis then turns to the efforts of the Italian state to fashion a unitary system by bureaucratic means, pulling authority from the periphery to the center and concentrating coordination in Rome in order to devise and apply uniform rules (Chapter 2). But bureaucratic controls are notably incomplete, even weak, with severe limits apparent even in the formal structure itself. The middle and most important chapter therefore concentrates on an alternative form of control—rule by professorial oligarchy. This form has its roots in the traditional position of the full professor on the Continent, the chair, a position that in Italy has been made into a tool of national power as well as elaborated at the local level, in formal and open ways as well as through informal and covert actions. The resulting particularism is a clear example of how a national effort to establish a bureaucratic framework for higher education can promote outcomes opposite to what was intended. Along the way, I describe features of the academic career in Italy and suggest what it has been like to be a student in the system.

With traditional structure identified and characterized, I discuss in Chapter 4 the possibilities and realities of reform, a matter to which Italy, like most other major nations, began to turn its attention in the 1960s. Change in the Italian system comes about through political incrementalism that may gradually alter the power structure while introducing bits and pieces of substantive reform. The political modes are heavily dominant over planning, bureaucratic intervention, professional raising of standards, and the leverage of competition and market forces.

The last chapter places the Italian case in a framework appropriate for cross-national analysis of the basic organization of the academic world. A relevant framework requires a clarification of the concept of the guild, since guild forms are still so prevalent, especially in academic systems based on the chair, and even, in muted fashion, in academic systems such as the American that have used the department as the primary operating unit and have given considerable power to administrators. In the vast commingling of authorities and types of authority that increasingly compose modern academic systems, the guild, in modern dress, is still to be reckoned with. Its forms have function as well as history. In Italy, we see a striking example of how the oldest precepts for the organization of academic work have endured in the twentieth century, as those who are thereby served have carried them inside the modern administrative state.

One
UNIVERSITY

It is, then, in institutions that the university tradition is most direct. First, the very name university, as an association of masters and scholars leading the common life of learning. Characteristic of the Middle Ages as such a corporation is, the individualistic modern world has found nothing to take its place.

Charles Homer Haskins, *The Rise of Universities*

In the beginning there was Bologna, an autonomous "university of students" so unhierarchical, so democratic that it could have occurred in the late Middle Ages only in one of the Italian city-states then in the midst of an intellectual and political renaissance.[1] Like the twentieth, the twelfth century placed new demands on education; a need for order in commerce and government in Italy, following upon a revival of trade and town life, called for fruitful knowledge, for educated men who would be something other than churchmen or soldiers—who would be, in particular, lawyers and administrators.[2] Individual scholars at the time were also developing a self-interest in systematizing the study of law and wished to separate it from general learning so that it might have the full attention of special groups of learners. Most of the students of the first clusters that were to become the University of Bologna were ecclesiastics and sons of nobles, mature young men of means who came to the city of Bologna from throughout Europe primarily to study law with private teachers of growing fame. There, as aliens lacking the civil rights of Bolognese, these students struggled to create an intentional community—to obtain, through concerted action, temporary citizenship, protection against landlords and other natural adversaries in the town, resources to hire teachers, and a united front that could hold the instructors accountable.[3]

In the society of the time, an established way of organizing voluntarily was at hand. This was the guild: "The university, whether of masters or of students, was only a particular kind of *guild*."[4] The new learning that was being initiated in the twelfth and thirteenth centuries could have quickly perished if it were not embodied in serviceable organization. The guild thus became the organizational base, the carrying mechanism for the idea of the university that was to endure for centuries.

The new ambition that flowered in Bologna rapidly caught on elsewhere in Italy; the time had come for the idea and the form. As groups of advanced teachers and learners formed in other Italian cities, they too took to the guild, partly in imitation of Bologna but also because it was an organizational mode that effectively served self-interest. Try as they might to secularize and specialize, the existing cathedral schools and monasteries were not sufficient to the needs of the emerging specialist groups in such fields as medicine and philosophy.[5] Guild organization was permitted, even encouraged, in the local settings in which the new clusters nested. Municipal authorities, for reasons of prestige and business, sought to attract students and teachers in the new academic specialties and thereby set in motion a dynamic of civic pride and competition. In the search for competitive advantage, a city would even offer exemption from military service or, further, citizenship and a subsidized bookshop.[6] Students and teachers alike were in a position to bargain sharply with city fathers, since they had a mobile form of what today would be called a university without walls. Holding lessons in the houses of the masters or in rented space, the scholars could pack up and leave whenever the host city became inhospitable or another city dangled alluring bait. Especially when murder or rent extortion was in the air, off they went—from Bologna to Modena, Reggio, Vicenza, Arezzo, Padua—to establish new universities, some of which were to perish while others proved indestructible.[7]

If the emerging academic guilds offered some autonomy, first for small groups and then for large numbers of teachers and students, they always fell within larger frameworks of church and state to which they had to adjust. In the medieval context, the church claimed primacy of control and by papal bulls in the thirteenth and fourteenth centuries attempted to bring the new academic corporations of Italy into a broad ecclesiastical system.[8] The major public authorities of the day entered the power equation as the source of all official licenses—therefore as the rightful center of regulation of the right to teach—and they sought to use the academic guilds as they did other guilds in the maintenance of public order. Thus, the problems of university autonomy and university-state relationships emerged as soon as the university became a distinguishable form of social organization.

Moreover, as different interests found use for the new way to organize the highest levels of learning, various forms of university authority soon obtained in Italy. An emperor (Frederick II) founded a university in Naples in 1224 and a pope (Innocent IV) set up a university in 1245 that traveled with his court.[9] Naturally, the institutions established by such powerful figures were vulnerable to arbitrary authority and hence somewhat different from the early student-organized clust_rs and the faculty guilds.

THE CONTRIBUTIONS OF EIGHT CENTURIES

Foremost in the historical legacy of the modern Italian university system was the guild organization, which initially took the unusual form of student organization dominating faculty organization. (In Paris and elsewhere in Europe scholars also turned to the guild, but in those places faculty-controlled guilds were predominant from the beginning.)

Student and Faculty Guilds

It now seems remarkable that the much-imitated Bologna model gave students so much influence in so many places, for a period stretching over three centuries. Student power, fueled by the need of alien students to protect themselves, was aided by the maturity, high social status, and political sophistication with which they were equipped. Their capacity to move from one city to another, and to move among instructors, made them men, not boys, in the threats and exchanges that are part of the exercise of political power: "Townsmen and professors alike stood in awe of a body [the students] which by the simple expedient of migration could destroy the trade of the former and the incomes of the latter."[10] However, these sources of student power were not to last. In the fifteenth and sixteenth centuries, the universities of Italy took up lasting residence in buildings.[11] Alien students became less important, as home-town boys went to the university, which was now geographically rooted. The towns, no longer to be intimidated by threats of secession, took over basic control from without, while the masters, now permanently employed by the state, were no longer dependent on students and student approval for their income.[12] What had been an essentially commercial relationship between buyers and sellers of a service was replaced by a more hierarchical one, based on state support of the professor, in which the consuming student was now subordinate.[13]

Thus, after reigning for several centuries, student corporations declined as faculty guilds ascended. Future power struggles involved clusters of teachers against officials of the supporting states and sometimes of the church. In retrospect, one might ask why the cities should have granted considerable power to the professors. Part of the answer is found in the weakness of state bureaucracy at a time when kings were not yet masters of their kingdoms, or city fathers of their communes. City and territorial governments in Italy, whether republican or despotic, were heavily dependent on semiautonomous groups: family groups or clans, political parties, and guilds, the latter organizing and supervising domains of work and participating in political power.[14] In their medieval setting and form, occupational guilds wielded enormous social and spiritual authority over their members. The guilds "exacted oaths of fealty, they had laws and jurisdiction, assemblies and officials, and in certain cases they established military or para-military formations."[15] Nominally subordinate, they were practically rival corporations to the state, and often they were more powerful than the state.[16] The guilds were part of a persisting substructure, extending from family to party, that was to cause Italian political life to remain for centuries "an invincible confusion."[17] And the guilds of higher learning, though they did not have troops, undoubtedly had great advantage in their control of training in advanced skills needed by government. Mystification of their craft proceeded apace.

The guild organization of the faculty that was to persist as a lasting note, from the fifteenth century on, had some feudal qualities. The division of labor depended on personal agreements among a small number of individuals; authority tended to be treated as a private possession; the essential relation between superiors and subordinates, masters and learners, was "not that between ruler and subject, nor state and citizen, but between lord and vassal."[18] We later emphasize that the personal control of professors has been high in the modern Italian university, with its immediate determinants located in the present structure of the system. But such control echos in a deep well of time, with centuries of higher learning offering resonance for a modern mode.

Identification with Cities

If internally the Italian university was historically rooted in the guild, externally it was rooted in the important cities of the peninsula. The rulers of the cities became, if not always the principal initiators, the primary patrons of the universities. Italian higher education never moved toward the isolation of the countryside, as happened so often in American higher education, but always located in an urban center. The university took its name from the city (Bologna, Pisa, Padua, Florence, Naples) and never, except for one or two minor instances in the twentieth century, from a private donor or higher public authority.

As the histories of the university and the containing city became intertwined over centuries, the Italian universities became deeply identified with specific places. Professors often became important local figures as they came to fill such roles as advisors to city governments, causing students to complain—as early as 1280 in Western history!—that their teachers were involved in outside affairs to the neglect of their academic duties.[19] When professors became famous, they contributed reputation and honor to the cities to which their universities were attached. Personal and institutional identities thereby became closely intertwined with the identities of cities: one would expect Naples, the university, to be unruly because of the "chaotic" nature of the city of Naples. And commonly whatever money and moral support was forthcoming from constituted authority came from city government, or from the provincial ruler who made the city his governmental center, rendering the universities party to some state supervision.[20] Thus connected to the city-state, the Italian university was a "state university" as early as the fifteenth century.

With the city as the principal environmental vessel, civic influences were early established in the history of the Italian university as more potent than church control. The Catholic church had its day, as during the Counter-Reformation, but as a large controlling framework it commonly ran second best to the civic authorities who paid the salaries and the bills. Despite the common perception from abroad of Italy as church-ridden in all matters, the Italian university was less influenced by religious forces than was American higher education until the twentieth century. In the United States, ministers and religious laymen long served as the dominant force on boards of trustees of colleges. Until the last half of the nineteenth century, when they were gradually replaced by secular businessmen and when presidents and faculties developed more power vis-à-vis the supervising trustees, "religious" trustees could, and did, question closely the religious purity of the staff and fire presidents and faculty who did not measure up to their own sectarian standards.[21] The faculty had no protection through guild rights and privileges.

In Italy, church influence on the universities was not based on immediate positions of control and supervision but on tenuous, indirect lines. In his classic review of the first four centuries of the growth of universities in the Western world, Hastings Rashdall concluded that, in Italy, the state triumphed over the church as the power to which academics could be forced to pay attention.[22]

A historian of schools and universities during the time of the Reformation has noted that the Italian universities were "virtually independent of Church control and lacking important theological faculties" and has concluded that, for all of Europe but especially Italy, "the most significant single aspect of education in this period is the way it fell increasingly under the control of the secular authority, council or prince."[23] More generally, historians of Italian city government maintain that Italians long ago in their civic life learned how to be religious without being churchly. Eric Cochrane, in his masterful study of Florence in the sixteenth to eighteenth centuries, has noted that the Florentines were possessed by a religiosity that was matched only by their anticlericalism; the behavior of monks and priests, which Boccaccio had once passed off as funny, was no longer amusing to the Florentines.[24] In the nineteenth century, too, the founders of the modern Italian national state were more opponents of the church than arms of its hegemony. It was state control rather than ecclesiastical control that the twelfth to the nineteenth centuries projected into the modern period of the Italian university.

Stagnation

When we attempt to determine the course of the Italian university after the fifteenth century, historical scholarship is so fragmentary and incomplete that we can only glance at the surface of events.[25] In the sixteenth and seventeenth centuries, there undoubtedly remained much that was impressive. The University of Padua, under the protection of Venice, was a great center of European medicine and possessed such luminaries in science as Copernicus and Vesalius. Pisa could claim Galileo as a medical student. But despite the famous names, the universities were being bypassed by one major development after another. The Italian city-states had begun to decline and the center of gravity in European university life slowly shifted northward to France and England. In Matthew Arnold's judgment, "The organized official teaching of Italy remained medieval and barbarous long after her great writers and artists had launched their country, and Europe along with her, on the line of modern ideas and modern civilization."[26]

Doctrinal rigidity became one of the important retarding forces. The established academic guilds were philosophically centered on a scholasticism—"Averroism"—that clung to a third-hand interpretation of Aristotle. But, most important, the Italian universities, like their counterparts elsewhere in Europe, had long been committed primarily to the preparation of lawyers, doctors, and civil servants, and were internally organized around professional studies. The general scholastic or humanistic doctrines that succeeded one another as gospel were considered appropriate for the training of professionals. Around the few professional fields, faculty established tight boundaries. Indeed, the most important trend of the sixteenth to eighteenth centuries in the universities of Italy, France, and Spain seems to have been toward a monopoly by the law faculty and the study of law alone.[27] All else was peripheral. This extremely narrow version of the university was characterized by maximum rigidity; it was an *ancien régime* unable to adapt imaginatively to new forces.

The Italian university proved especially hostile to science, the most important force for change after the fifteenth century.[28] Able to secure only a marginal place within the university, scientific groups developed new and intellectually more congenial institutions, such as the court-sponsored academies and clusters that, for a while in Italy, so creatively grouped scientists, engineers, and artists. In Urbino and Milan, Florence and Rome, these external clusters supported many of the geniuses of Italian art and science. All small in size by present standards, several of these institutions contained a density of talent seemingly never later surpassed in the history of man, including the scientific laboratories of the twentieth century. As early as the fifteenth century, under such sponsorship as that of Federigo of Monte-feltro, Duke of Urbino, and Lorenzo de' Medici, Duke of Florence, such towering figures as Piero della Francesca, Michelangelo, and Leonardo da Vinci did much of their work.

From such small bases, a distinct scientific identity and role emerged in Europe in the seventeenth century. But even in the most congenial settings the prospects for science were always bleaker in Italy than in northern Europe. One reason lay in the connection of science to supporting interests. A growing middle class in a more fluid structure in the north found practical returns from the support of science, whereas in Italy the support of science continued in the upper-class circles of sponsorship whose fundamental interests remained conservative in politics and humanistic in intellectual matters. As put by Joseph Ben-David: "In other parts of Europe the cause of science was taken up by a class of persons who stood to gain from changes in the social order. In Italy by contrast, science became, by the sixteenth century, the concern of a minority within a class which had attained what it wanted and which was interested in social stability."[29] Religion also played a part, with the thought and structure of Protestantism, and the interests of certain Protestant groups, more favorable to science than was Catholicism.

The fate of science in Italy in the fifteenth to eighteenth centuries—the reconquest of science by the nonscientific culture, as Ben-David has called it[30]—is the best clue to the general character of the Italian universities during this period. More than in northern Europe, they remained tied to their medieval origins. The faculties that had developed out of the earlier period remained strongly entrenched in guild organization. "The cities had continued to be small and closed political units composed of guilds carefully isolated from one another and graded by legal privilege and traditional values."[31] The universities partook of this general style. If eighteenth-century guilds in western Europe were the epitome of "purely obstructive monopoly,"[32] their great remaining strength in the fragmented political and social structure of Italy made them a central factor in the conditions that were pushing that formerly powerful peninsula to the periphery of European affairs. The Italian universities, locked into this general resistance to change, moved to the margin of European intellectual life as they retained the character of small and isolated units interested in and defending only a few segments of professional preparation. They could handle the education neither of a "gentleman-ruler"—idealized in the new elites of the Renaissance—nor of the increasing numbers of experts and amateurs who were adopting the modern belief in scientific research.[33]

Whatever the full mixture of such causes as the general

economic decline of the supporting cities,[34] the assault of wars and foreign occupations,[35] the repression of scholarship in a censorious Counter-Reformation, the internal rigidity of centuries-old organization, by the eighteenth century the Italian universities were relatively weak in comparison with their strength in the thirteenth and fourteenth centuries and with that of their counterparts in northern Europe in the later period.[36]

Other scattered bits of information suggest that the remote past of the Italian universities was a glorious time compared to more recent centuries. The great age of university founding in Italy fell before 1400. Leaving aside the institutions that did not continue into the present period and looking only at universities existing in 1960, we find amazing antiquity: over two-thirds were established before 1600, and more were founded in the fourteenth century than in the nineteenth and twentieth centuries combined (table 1). Moreover, of the nine major university centers that produce most of the academics of the country today,[37] eight date from before 1500. Only Milan came later, in the twentieth century, leaving a gap of four centuries during which no important universities were established.

Enrollments, too, reveal gradual decline over recent centuries. The venerable University of Bologna, reporting students in the thousands in the thirteenth century, was down to two to three hundred in the eighteenth and nineteenth centuries.[38] A Bologna faculty of one hundred sixty professors in the seventeenth century fell away to sixty a hundred years later.[39] Young English gentlemen of the eighteenth and nineteenth centuries might make a grand tour in Italy to sow some wild oats, bask in the sun, and enjoy the monuments, but they and their peers of the Continental north no longer went there for formal learning as had once been true. In all the countries of Western Europe, the clientele for higher education was more likely to stay at home as national states developed. But for those who were determined to find the best instruction, it was to France, Germany, and England that they went. The Italian system fell out of contention as a major center of the higher learning.

The Italian universities thus survived the eighteenth and nineteenth centuries but with weakened viability and greatly diminished international standing. When Italy's educational system was recently ranked among those of some seventy-five

TABLE 1: ITALIAN STATE UNIVERSITIES, 1960, BY DATE OF ORIGIN

Before 1600		After 1600	
Date of Origin	University	Date of Origin	University
12th century		17th century	
1158	Bologna	1606	Cagliari
1175	Modena		
		18th century	
13th century		1727	Camerino
1222	Padua	1773	Genoa
1224	Naples		
1246	Siena	19th century[a]	
		1806	Palermo
14th century			
1303	Rome	20th century	
1308	Perugia	1923	Milan
1343	Pisa	1924	Bari
1349	Florence	1924	Trieste
1361	Pavia		
1391	Ferrara		
15th century			
1405	Turin		
1444	Catania		
16th century			
1512	Parma		
1540	Macerata		
1548	Messina		
1562	Sassari		

SOURCES: Universities, especially the ancient ones, are often unsure of their age or undependable in reporting it. They evolved out of predecessor schools and colleges and hence birth was a prolonged affair; they received official recognition decades, and sometimes centuries, after the time they believe they were "founded." They have a self-interest in stretching the truth about how old they are and whether they were ever out of commission for a while and had to start over again. Hence, different records and source books do not always agree with reported dates of origin differing from a few years to several centuries. Rashdall, *The Universities of Europe*, has been used as the most dependable source for origins before 1500, the date when his admirable coverage ends, and also for placing the beginning of Parma as a recognized university in 1512. The *International Handbook of Universities*, pp. 550–73, has been used for origins since that time.
a. Two polytechnic institutes in Turin and Milan, now supported by the national government and considered institutions of university rank, were initiated in 1859 and 1863.

countries in the mid-twentieth century, it appeared in a "semi-advanced" category, on a level with the systems of Hungary, Poland, and Yugoslavia.[40] Based on enrollments in secondary and higher education, this crude rating was not inappropriate in placing Italy a step down from all the countries of northern Europe, which were placed in an "advanced" category despite highly restricted levels of participation at the advanced educational levels.

SHAPE OF THE TWENTIETH-CENTURY UNIVERSITY
Broad Purposes
The structure of the Italian university as of 1960, whatever its limitations, expressed traditional European notions of the purposes and forms of higher education.

Throughout Europe, higher education has been viewed as a place for professional training and specialization. Students have completed their general education by the time they leave the secondary school and are ready to specialize, much as American students do upon choosing a major at the beginning of their junior year of college and, more so, at entry to graduate or professional school. The university has not needed to concern itself with general programs that would cause students to distribute effort among the humanities, the arts, the social sciences, and the natural sciences. Rather, the student tunnels into a specialty by enrolling in a particular faculty and concentrating, often, in a part of it, again much like graduate students in the American system.

Upon the completion of programs of study that vary between four and six years in different fields, the Italian student receives the *laurea*, a degree considered by Italians to be higher than the American bachelor's and more on a par with the American master's degree. Whatever its repute, the *laurea* monopolizes certification. There is little available below or above it: only a few diplomas for completion of shorter programs in a few fields and no higher degree like the Ph.D. to certify completion of post-graduate work. This economy in certification of graduates also fits the Italian (and more generally European) traditional conception of the functions of higher education. As only a small proportion of the young proceed past the secondary level, an elite has already been separated from the mass. That small group can then be trained for the professions and public administration, and, if needed, for the private business sector. For purposes of social differentiation, there is no compelling reason why the educated group needs two or three degree levels. One degree, the *laurea*, can serve as the basic credential for higher positions.

The forms and procedures of Italian higher education also mesh with traditional understandings of what professors and students should do. By tradition the professor is to present lectures during the year and to give examinations periodically. As students have completed their general education, the professor need not be concerned with character building or with any conception of education that requires attention to students outside the classroom. In fact, professors need hardly concern themselves with how much students participate in lectures and laboratory, since the Continental tradition assigns to students the responsibility to pick up the specialized knowledge that will enable them to pass the examinations. The loose relationship between professors and students, entailing much discretion on both sides, can function with a relatively small senior staff of lecturing professors. It can entail a high student-teacher ratio in many fields, one that not only reflects the many seats of the lecture hall but also the fact that, when many students do not attend lectures, course enrollment can be allowed to outnumber seats by a wide margin.

The simple Italian structure has also expressed a European conception of university organization that radically subordinates administration. Since admissions are decided at the time of leaving the secondary school and not at the door of the university, no admissions office has been necessary. Without *in loco parentis* responsibility for students or even for their steady attendance and progress, the university has had little need of deans of students, house mothers and house masters, testing officers, and guidance personnel. With funds fixed in governmental budgets, public relations and fund raising have little urgency. And since Continental universities have managed to do without intercollegiate athletics, they do not require athletic directors, coaches, alumni representatives, and ushers for the stadium. In academic matters, councils of professors run things within the faculties, leaving only some bookkeeping to be done by a few university administrators. The superstructure of administration found in U.S.

universities has had only a small counterpart in Italy, as elsewhere on the Continent. The traditional university did not require
it.[41]

The Context of Elite Selection

Compared to even the sharply tapered educational pyramids of
France, Germany, Belgium, and Sweden, the set of universities
found in Italy at the midpoint of the twentieth century presented
a solid case of elite educational structure, with only small
proportions of the relevant age group entering and graduating.
As late as 1960, only about 5 to 6 percent of this age group (the
nineteen- to twenty-five-year-olds) were enrolled (the U.S. rate in
that year was some four times higher).[42] In a nation of fifty
million people university students numbered about 240,000 in
1950 and 280,000 in 1960.[43] There was also a high dropout rate;
only about one in twenty-five young adults, or 4 percent, completed the university and obtained the degree.[44] This low "output" figure, perhaps the most important single indicator of elite
higher education, was on a par with the lowest among the rest of
the countries of western Europe.[45] It was about equal to the
completion rate in American higher education about the time of
World War I.

Yet the sharpest divide in the educational ladder has until
recently been between the elementary and secondary levels.
Primary education was deemed sufficient for the masses whereas
secondary education served as a highly selective gateway to higher
education. But mass schooling even at the elementary and middle
school (junior high school) levels did not come into being until
after World War II, reaching 80 percent of the age group as late
as 1950 and 90 percent in 1960. The young did not stay in school
in significant proportions above these lower levels, that is, after
the age of fourteen. Only 10 percent of the young who were
fourteen to eighteen years of age were in secondary education in
1950; in 1960, the numbers had risen only to the still-low
proportion of 20 percent.[46] It was not until the 1960s that Italy
moved into mass secondary education. As a result of the late
arrival of mass education, the Italian population of the postwar
period has been poorly schooled. In 1960, the median level of
education of Italian adults was about five years of school, or at a
point slightly lower than that of adults in the United States in
1920, forty years earlier.[47]

The actual completion of school grades by Italian children has been below what even the low rates of participation would suggest, since Italian teachers traditionally have flunked large numbers and held them back in the grades. Only about 50 percent of the young were actually completing their primary education in 1960, despite participation rates of 80 and 90 percent.[48] Only about 25 percent finished the work of the middle schools, and, still in 1960, only 13 percent graduated from the upper secondary school.[49]

In addition, the secondary level has contained several types of specialized schools that vary in capacity to qualify the young for higher education (table 2). A classical school (*liceo classico*), as in France, Germany, and Britain (in the form of its grammar school), has been traditionally the basic route to higher educa-

TABLE 2: SECONDARY SCHOOLS AND DIFFERENTIAL ADMISSION TO HIGHER EDUCATION, 1960

Type of Secondary School	First-Year Enrollment in Upper Secondary Schools, as Percentage of All Students	School Background of First-Year University Students, as Percentage of All Students
Classical liceo	14	46
Scientific liceo	7	15
Teacher-training school	13	15
Technical and vocational institutes	66	24
	100	100

SOURCE: Organization for Economic Co-operation and Development, *Reviews of National Policies for Education: Italy* (Paris: 1969), pp. 72, 77.

tion, offering access to nearly all parts of the university. A scientific school (*liceo scientifico*) has also led to most of the university disciplines, excluding chiefly the humanities. But other secondary schools that have historically specialized in the preparation of elementary-school teachers and in technical and vocational education have been largely terminal, offering only limited admission to a few university fields; for example, the graduates of the secondary school that prepared teachers (*Istituto Magistrale*) could enter only the Faculty of Education (*Magistero*).[50]

In sum, the Italian system has systematically and on a massive scale discouraged students from going on. In the light of strict norms of classical education, it has defined a large share of the school population as backward students.

The Units of Organization

To a degree not exceeded in any other major country the university form of organization has monopolized official higher education in Italy. In the mid-1960s, only a minuscule 2 percent of the higher education enrollment was outside the university,[51] in scattered schools of social work, teacher education, physical education, nautical studies, languages, and other applied subjects. In contrast, other countries have placed students to a greater degree in one or more nonuniversity sectors. In France, nonuniversity enrollment amounted to about 30 percent; in Germany, to about 40 percent; and in the United Kingdom to about 50 percent.[52] The nearest to Italy in this regard has been Sweden, where, in the mid-1960s, about 10 percent of the students were located in other units. In Italy anything that is important has been kept within the one sector. The country has developed two important polytechnical institutes in Milan and Turin, the latter also known as "Fiat University" because of its close connection to the Fiat firm. But because these two institutes are important they are treated as within the set of universities, operated accordingly, and so counted in statistics. Thus with no major separate technological sector, as in Germany and Britain, or a major group of teacher-training colleges, as in Britain and the United States, the country has essentially left higher education to the university alone.

Further restriction of form is found in the extent to which the universities come under one general type of support and supervision. After the unification of the nation, almost all the major universities were designated as public universities to be financed in considerable part by the national government. Of the approximately thirty universities found in the country in the early 1960s, twenty-four were national public universities and only six were in a residual "free" sector where control rested with municipal sponsorship or was private in the American sense. Only one under mainly municipal support, the University of Urbino, was of considerable size and importance, and only two private institutions, Luigi Bocconi and the Catholic University of Milan, were noteworthy for quality or for size, status, and power.

Secular or religious, the few institutions in the "free" sector have not been independent of the public framework, since they are subject to many of the rules and regulations operative in the public set of institutions. Public regulation is grounded in the fact that the only valued degree is the state-approved *laurea*. Here then is another element of monopolization: the predominance of a national public system, with only a minor private sector. In Italy there are no powerful enterprises historically molded outside the control of the state, in the style of Oxford and Cambridge in England and Harvard and Yale and other major private institutions in the United States.

Characteristics of the University Units

Though higher education in Italy is highly homogeneous in organizational form—the university alone, offering one degree, under support and supervision of the national government—Italian universities are hardly of a piece, even in the most obvious structural characteristics. For one, they vary greatly in size. A few are gigantic, whereas others remain too small to be universities other than in name.

Size. In 1960, fourteen universities, or about half of the total number, had 8,000 students or more (table 3). The University of Rome was the giant, with about 45,000 students, followed by Naples with 28,000, and the University of Bari, a relatively new institution (1924) in the deep south of the peninsula, with 16,000 students. As expansion took hold in Italian higher education, all of these fourteen large institutions, save the Catholic University in the free sector, at least doubled in size in the decade of the sixties. By 1970 Rome had 89,000 students, Naples had 60,000, and Bari had 37,000.

Considerably smaller were seven institutions, here grouped as medium-size, that in 1960 had between 3,500 and 5,000 students each: among the state universities, Pavia, Perugia, Parma, Trieste, and Cagliari (Sardinia); among the free universities, the privately supported Bocconi in Milan and the municipally supported university in Urbino. These institutions also all grew in size in the 1960s, to range between 5,000 and 16,000 students by the end of the decade. Although the rate of growth was high, in absolute numbers they were not growing on a par with the large universities.

TABLE 3: UNIVERSITIES BY SIZE OF STUDENT ENROLLMENT

	Enrollment				
University	1960	1965	1970	5-year Increase, 1960–65	10-year Increase, 1960–70
Large (over 8,000)					
Rome	45,000	58,000	89,000	13,000	44,000
Naples	28,000	37,000	60,000	9,000	32,000
Bari	16,000	28,000	37,000	12,000	21,000
Bologna	15,000	22,000	36,000	7,000	21,000
Palermo	14,000	16,000	31,000	2,000	17,000
Milan:					
Catholic[a]	12,000	18,000	21,000	6,000	9,000
Genoa	11,000	14,000	24,000	3,000	13,000
Turin	10,000	16,000	28,000	6,000	18,000
Padua	10,000	17,000	27,000	7,000	17,000
Florence	9,000	13,000	25,000	4,000	16,000
Pisa	9,000	14,000	23,000	5,000	14,000
Messina	9,000	14,000	25,000	5,000	16,000
Milan:					
State	8,000	11,000	26,000	3,000	18,000
Catania	8,000	12,000	21,000	4,000	13,000
(Average increase)				(6,000)	(19,000)
Medium (3,000–8,000)					
Milan:					
Bocconi[a]	5,000	6,700	5,100	1,700	100
Parma	4,800	7,600	14,200	2,800	9,400
Cagliari	4,400	8,400	14,800	4,000	10,400
Pavia	4,300	6,600	11,200	2,300	6,900
Urbino[a]	4,200	7,000	8,400	2,800	4,200
Perugia	4,100	7,400	15,800	3,300	11,700
Trieste	3,500	5,700	8,800	2,200	5,300
(Average increase)				(2,700)	(6,900)

(TABLE 3, CONTINUED)

	Enrollment				
University	1960	1965	1970	5-year Increase, 1960-65	10-year Increase, 1960-70
Small (less than 3,000)					
Modena	2,700	3,200	5,100	500	2,400
Ferrara	2,000	2,600	4,500	600	2,500
Sassari	1,400	1,800	3,700	400	2,300
Siena	1,200	2,000	5,200	800	4,000
Camerino	1,000	1,400	1,800	400	800
Lecce[a]	900	3,100	6,800	2,200	5,900
Aquila[a]	800	3,000	6,000	2,200	5,200
Macerata	700	1,100	1,800	400	1,100
Chieti[a]	— [b]	370	1,700	—	—
(Average increase)				(900)	(3,000)

SOURCE: Italy, Istituto centrale di statistica, *Annuario statistico dell'istruzione italiana*, vol. 24, pp. 320-21.
NOTE: Universities are listed in order of size in 1960-61. The enrollment figures include *fuori corso* (out-of-course) students, i. e., those who have not completed their work in the normal number of years but continue to register with the hope of yet passing the examinations and other requirements. This category has been regularly used in showing enrollment in Italian universities. The enrollments have been rounded to the nearest 1,000 among the large universities; to the nearest 100 among the medium and small universities.
a. "Free," or nonstate, institution.
b. Not founded until after 1960.

Finally, in 1960 there were nine units called universities that had less than 3,000 students; some had even less than 1,000—about the size of a small private liberal arts college in the United States. All these small institutions grew in the sixties, two of them at a rapid rate: Aquila, from 800 to 5,200, and Lecce, from 900 to 5,900. But again the increase in absolute numbers was small compared to that of the giant institutions. Over the decade, then, there was a growing disparity in size: the increase in students averaged 19,000 in the large institutions, 7,000 in the middle-size category, and 3,000 in the small.

Location. Any consideration of the geographic distribution of the universities turns early to fundamental differences, rooted deep in history, between northern and southern Italy—the more forward-looking, progressive, industrialized north of Turin, Milan, and Bologna, and the backward and depressed south of Naples, the southern mainland, Sicily, and Sardinia. In discussions of Italian higher education the charge is sometimes made that the north has more than its share of university places for students whereas the south is grossly underrepresented. The actual situation has inclined in that direction but not radically so. In the early 1960s the south (below Rome, plus Sicily and Sardinia) contained about 38 percent of the population.[53] It contained eight universities (table 4), or about a fourth of the total, compared to ten universities in central Italy (Florence to Rome) and twelve in the north (above Florence). But the south had more than its share of the large universities: in Naples and Bari, it had two of the three largest, and, with Palermo added, three of the top five. Sicily was not badly provided for, since it

TABLE 4: UNIVERSITIES BY GEOGRAPHICAL DISTRIBUTION AND SIZE, 1960

Region	Size		
	Large	Medium	Small
North	Bologna Milan: Catholic[a] Turin Padua Genoa Milan: State	Milan: Luigi Bocconi[a] Parma Pavia Trieste	Modena Ferrara
Central	Rome Florence Pisa	Urbino[a] Perugia	Siena Camerino Aquila[a] Macerata Chieti[a]
South	Naples Bari Palermo Messina Catania	Cagliari	Sassari Lecce[a]

NOTE: "North," above Florence; "Central," Florence to Rome; "South," below Rome plus Sicily and Sardinia. Size categories and university size based on 1960 data and categories shown in table 3.
a. "Free," or nonstate, institution.

had three large universities (Palermo, Messina, and Catania), and the island of Sardinia had two, one medium size (Cagliari) and one small (Sassari). Thus, in the 1960s about a third of all Italian students were in the southern universities, a figure close to the proportion of southerners in the population.[54] There has been, however, some deprivation in parts of the south in geographic accessibility. Until very recently the south lacked university sites chiefly in the provinces of Calabria and Basilicata, in the toe and instep of the foot of the peninsula (see map).[55]

Characteristics of the Faculty Units

Within the universities, the fields are assembled in faculties (*Facoltà*), which are the primary units for membership and participation and the major organizational divisions inside the universities. Professors and assistants hold appointment in a faculty and carry out their duties almost completely within it. A student enrolls in a faculty and typically takes all classes there. The student is examined by a part of the faculty and finally is approved for the degree by the faculty. The faculties have been so much the inclusive settings for teaching and learning that even in small universities it has not been thought essential to unite them on a "campus." They are often dispersed in different parts of a city, whether in Milan or Florence or Naples, or even in Rome, where Mussolini attempted to build a central campus but simply left some *Facoltà* saddled with horrible architecture. What has counted is not the unity of the university but the availability of different degree opportunities within a given city as provided by the existence there of appropriate faculties.

In most cases, the faculty centers on a professional field of study and can be roughly likened to a professional school in American universities. The important difference is that in Italy, as elsewhere on the Continent, a student enters the professional specialty directly after leaving the secondary school, whereas in the United States a student commonly takes four undergraduate years and a bachelor's degree between high school and professional study in such fields as medicine, law, or architecture.

There are nine professional faculties in the Italian universities: medicine, law, engineering, economics and commerce (devoted mainly to the latter and to preparation for business careers), agriculture, teaching, veterinary medicine, architecture, and

Italian Universities, State and "Free,"
by Geographical Distribution and Size, 1960

● 8,000 or more students
⊙ 3,000–8,000 students
· less than 3,000 students
✳ "Free," or nonstate, institution

pharmacy. Three other faculties—in letters, science, and political science—organize what in the United States would be segments of the liberal arts, that is, the set of disciplines in the humanities, the social sciences, and the natural sciences that make up the liberal arts undergraduate college and the graduate school. The medical faculties offer a six-year course of study, engineering and architecture a five-year program, and all the other faculties, mainly a four-year curriculum.

Within the faculties, fields of study come under the administration of chairs, the positions of full professors. Since the chairs are the basic units of senior staffing and the operations of the teaching program, their sheer number in various faculties roughly indicates the relative size and strength of the faculties. For example, in 1958, all the faculties of medicine in Italy contained 440 chairs, whereas the faculties of pedagogy (*Magistero*) possessed only 65; law had 326, whereas pharmacy had 31 (table 5).

In number of chairs, the faculties could be divided into a big six and a small six. The big six, in descending order, were medicine, law, science, letters, engineering, and economics. The three fields of medicine, law, and engineering together had about half of all the full professors in the country; medicine alone had one-fifth. The small six were agriculture, teaching, veterinary medicine, political science, architecture, and pharmacy.

Relative strength of the major fields is also reflected in the average number of chairholders found in the faculties that represent the fields throughout the country. In 1960, medicine was both widely distributed in the nation in the form of twenty-one faculties, and had the formidable strength of averaging twenty-one chairs per faculty. Law possessed twenty-six faculties, the largest number of any field, with an average of a dozen chairholding professors per faculty. In contrast, teaching and pharmacy, although widely distributed geographically, in twenty and twenty-three faculties respectively, were weak in averaging only about three chairs for teaching and one and one-half chairs for pharmacy per faculty. Political science was found in only six places throughout all of Italy, and averaged eight chairs; the study of architecture was carried by seven faculties with an average of six chairholders per faculty. Clearly the Italian universities have not had a standard composition of faculties, let alone faculties of comparable size.

TABLE 5: FIELDS OF STUDY BY SIZE IN CHAIRS AND FACULTIES, 1958-60

Field of Study	No. of Chairholders	No. of Faculties	Chairs per Faculty
Big Six			
Medicine	440	21	21.0
Law	326	26	12.5
Science	299	23[a]	13.0
Letters	299	20	15.0
Engineering	175	13	13.5
Economics	149	19	7.8
Small Six			
Agriculture	102	13	7.8
Teaching	65	20[b]	3.3
Veterinary Medicine	62	9	6.9
Political Science	47	6[c]	7.8
Architecture	39	7	5.6
Pharmacy	31	23	1.3
Total	2034	200	

SOURCES: Comitato di studio dei problemi dell'Università italiana, *Studi sull'Università italiana*, vol. I, *La popolazione universitaria*, p. 219; Italy, Istituto centrale di statistica, *Annuario statistico dell'istruzione italiana*, vol. 14.
a. 22 Faculties of Science, plus 1 Faculty of Industrial Chemistry.
b. 19 Faculties of Pedagogy, plus the Oriental Institute of Naples.
c. 5 Faculties of Political Science, plus 1 Faculty of Statistical Science.

There is great variation in the educational assembly not only in terms of the internal composition of the individual universities but also in terms of the major cities as educational sites where there may be more than one university. A few universities have had all, or nearly all, of the dozen different faculties. In 1960, the University of Rome had all twelve faculties, and the University of Naples ten of them (table 6). In Milan the state university contained only six faculties, but Catholic University of Milan also had six, Luigi Bocconi had one (economics and commerce), and the Politechnic had two (engineering and architecture), giving the city of Milan fifteen faculties in eleven of the possible fields, lacking only pharmacy. In contrast to Rome or Naples or the Milan complex, many of the universities and university sites have only a few faculties. Ancient Siena, in the mid-twentieth century,

TABLE 6: NUMBER OF FACULTIES IN EACH UNIVERSITY, 1960

University	No. of Faculties	University	No. of Faculties
Full[a]		Partial[b]	
Rome	12	Parma	6
Bologna	11	Sassari	6
Florence	10	Urbino	5
Naples	10	Ferrara	4
Palermo	10	Modena	4
Turin	9		
Padua	9		
Pisa	9		
Bari	9	Nominal[c]	
Perugia	8	Siena	3
Messina	8	Camerino	3
Cagliari	8	Lecce	2
Trieste	7	Milan: Luigi	
Genoa	7	Bocconi	1
Catania	7	Aquila	1
Milan: State	6	Macerata	1
Milan: Catholic	6		
Pavia	6		

SOURCE: Italy, Istituto centrale di statistica, *Annuario statistico dell'istruzione italiana*, vol. 14.
a. Contain faculties in the four major fields of medicine, law, letters, and science.
b. Contain four faculties or more, in any fields of study, but not in all four major fields of medicine, law, letters, and science.
c. Contain three faculties or less.

had only law, medicine, and pharmacy. Tiny Macerata offered only law; Lecce had only letters and teaching; Modena had only the four fields of law, medicine, science, and pharmacy. Sassari, in Sardinia, with six faculties, had significant enrollment in only three (law, with 800 students; medicine, with 200; agriculture, with 200); its other three faculties (science, pharmacy, and veterinary medicine) enrolled thirty to sixty students each. Similarly, the universities have had radical differences in the number of chairholders. In the early 1960s, before student expansion brought increases in faculty size, the University of Rome already had about two hundred chairholders and the University of Naples one hundred and fifty; among the medium-size universities Cagliari had about sixty and Parma fifty; among the small ones,

Ferrara had thirty and Macerata ten.[56] The universities and faculties clearly were vastly different as assemblies of chair-based power.

Thus, the term "university" has embraced places differing widely in their coverage of studies. A university might *not* have a faculty of letters, covering the humanities, the arts, and part of the social sciences. Or, having letters, it might not have a science faculty. Moreover, some of the smaller universities, sharply limited in scope, offer neither field. If we search the landscape of Italian higher education for the presence of the four major fields of medicine, law, letters, and science, we find, in 1960, eighteen places that included at least the two most important professions together with much of letters and science (table 6). These we term full universities. Another five places may be considered partial universities: They contained at least four faculties of one kind or another but lacked one or more of the four primary fields. That leaves six places that contained three faculties or fewer; essentially these were universities in name only.

Fragmentation

As we have seen in this chapter, history and geography have both contributed to fragmentation among the Italian universities and their constituent parts. Thus the overriding organizational problem that the Italians have faced in higher education over the last hundred years has been that of forging a national system out of the many universities and faculties that have few discernible bonds. Summarized below, in order of increasing importance, are five of the major forces that have constrained efforts at system building.

Geographic spread. The Italian universities and faculties are physically scattered from the most eastern and western reaches of the north (Trieste and Turin), through isolated hill-towns as well as major cities in the center, to the bottom of the mainland boot and off on the islands of Sicily and Sardinia. For any purposes of systematic organization topped by central authority, these "field units" are truly off in the field, far out of sight of the center rather than grouped around it. This characteristic of geographic dispersion in a national service is shared with many other segments of national public administration in Italy and other countries that have branch locations outside the capital. Compared to that in the Soviet Union, the dispersion is minor; compared to that in Sweden and Belgium, it is major.

Regional differences. The scattered universities and faculties are located in regions that vary greatly in economic, political, and cultural character. Between north and south there has been a main point of cleavage, a massive obstacle to attempts to effect even minimal uniformity and equity in nationally administered sets of organizations. So long rooted in regions, the universities cannot help but be subjected to the strains of regional differences.

Identification with local city. Early established and long enduring, the connection of university and supporting city produced a joint pride of place long before Italy was made into a nation, a sense not to be easily dispersed by those who would summon a higher loyalty to a national identity. The place of Padua, the university, in the history and literature of the world is also the place of Padua the city. This type of local identification is a fundamental force that is contrary to principles of concerted action that lead to a national system.

Identification with institutional self. Beyond being identified with the city, the Italian university has been identified with itself. The general push for autonomy that is characteristic of universities is strengthened greatly when it is backed by a sense of distinctive institutional identity. In the historically renowned Italian universities, the symbolic side of organization has been powerful: Bologna, Perugia, Turin, Pavia—each has a cherished, richly embroidered place in history that is full of traditions, symbols, and myths. Bologna is able to claim first place in history, Dante and Petrarch as students—and then, for good measure, toss in the names of Boccaccio, Copernicus, Erasmus, and even Luther.[57] A high official in such a place can charm and stun a visitor in a few hours with an overload of the senses: a tour of lecture halls where legendary figures stood behind the lecterns in the seventeenth century; a view of towers and buildings whose lasting beauty dates from the fifteenth and sixteenth centuries and which have somehow survived the passing of so many generations of foreign conquest and civil strife; a gift of beautiful volumes that chronicle the great figures, the magnificent buildings, and the great moments in the long institutional history; and, finally, a presentation of the university medallion in an office graced with old books and tapestries. There is so much upon which to base institutional pride—and, of course, with which to divert the attention of the visitor from such symptoms of current problems as the broken glass and disfigured walls produced by a recent student action and the crumbling of buildings occasioned by misuse and neglect. It is difficult enough to line up new state colleges in an American state and ask them to resemble one another closely; it is another thing to make units in a system out of Italian universities whose sense of self has been elaborated in centuries of development that predated the system-making forces.

Guild understructure. Whatever the larger framework of state, church, and private sponsorship found in various places and times, the core organizational form in universities has been guildlike groupings of faculty members. In Italy and other Continental countries, the chair and the faculty are direct descendants of the guild. Their current modes of action are not identical with those of the past, and we later consider how they have changed. But the chair has continued to assert individual autonomy, and the faculty the self-rule of a group of peers. The individual university is a collection of units each more interested in maintaining its own autonony within the university than in weaving a larger fabric for a national system. Everywhere operative to some degree, this force of fragmentation is bound to be strong in a country where universities can claim connection with the life of the twelfth to sixteenth centuries, and are living evidence that they have endured, at their own level of organization, despite what has happened in the turmoil of the larger scene.

Thus, Italian universities are loaded with strong centrifugal forces that weaken the possibility of their behaving readily as linked parts of a whole. Those who have tried to make a national system of higher education in Italy have had somehow to knit together geographically dispersed institutions that are suffused with regional differences, wedded to local cities, full of historic pride, and composed of guildlike clusters. Coordinating the Italian universities was necessarily a major task for national administration. In the following chapter we explore how it was attempted.

Two
BUREAUCRACY

I cannot conceive that a nation can live and prosper without a powerful centralization of government. But I am of the opinion that a centralized administration is fit only to enervate the nations in which it exists, by incessantly diminishing their local spirit.

Alexis de Tocqueville, *Democracy in America*

System-building in higher education in Italy has been intimately a part of the making of a national state. For about a century, the universities have been officially under the direction of a central ministry of education, thereby constituting, at least formally, a sector of the executive branch of the government. In line with this structural position, Italian education in its entirety has long had the reputation of being heavily bureaucratized—even, like the French system, of being top-heavy in control from the center. Clearly, in a search for the ingredients of academic power, we should begin with the bureaucratic tool that the state has fashioned. What is the significance of the national administrative structure in the life of the Italian universities?

As we shall see, the paths of decision-making do indeed lead to Rome, within a general framework etched by bureaucratic methods. There have been official lines running to and from the national center in the operation of a national budget, a national curriculum, and a national assignment of personnel. These administrative patterns are themselves fascinating, since they are so different from what has obtained in the United States and Britain and other countries that concert higher education in formally more decentralized ways. In addition, there are general features of public administration in Italy that condition the educational realm as well as other governmental sectors. Even when the university sector appears to deviate radically from all other parts of government, the deviant pattern is usually an amalgam of conditions unique in higher education and ways common in Italian government. Some knowledge of the administrative environment helps to make sense of the Italian way in higher education. Whatever the features of French and German higher education that have been imitated in Italy, they have had to be adapted to Italian conditions, among which the nature of governmental administration has loomed large.

THE ADMINISTRATIVE SETTING

Alexis de Tocqueville, that great admirer of American federalism, may have early established (in the 1830s) the dictum that, while governments may centralize control and rule from the center, they ought not attempt to *administer* from the center.[1] But many elites have thought otherwise, including those that established the machinery of the modern Italian state.

Centralization and Concentration

To rule from the center is to centralize political control, moving authority from local and provincial government to the national level. To administer from the center is to concentrate authority in the central offices of the national agencies, instead of spreading it among field offices in the regions and localities. The tendency to do both has run deep in Italy.[2] Even before the Napoleonic absorption of much of the peninsula, the separate Italian states, controlled by absolutist regimes, were inclined to centralize and concentrate. The French forms of administration that were applied to much of Italy while Napoleon was in control (1792–1814) "represented only a rationalization of the centralizing machinery created by the former absolutist governments."[3] That "rationalization" was an extensive effort. In a unitary structure laid down on a large territory, authority extended from Napoleon himself in Paris to area prefects and down the line to the mayors of cities and towns now positioned as appointed officials of a supranational state. Local self-determination, at least formally, amounted to little compared to the power of the agents of the central executive.[4]

After the Napoleonic period, the peninsula fell again into its former splintered condition, divided into the eight separate states, or spheres of influence, established by the Congress of Vienna in 1815.[5] Most of them again became absolute monarchies but now they were better schooled in how to concentrate administration as well as to centralize political control. In each, a number of central ministries, commonly seven or eight, developed around such major concerns as foreign affairs, finance, and justice; and, at least three of the states (Piedmont, Tuscany, and the Two Sicilies) organized a Ministry of Public Instruction.[6]

The Piedmontese of the Turin area in the north, who led later in the making of the nation, set the pace in administrative matters. When they brought their own monarchy into a constitutional form in 1848, placing an elected chamber alongside a royally appointed senate, they sought to make their own centralized administrative machinery a model for the other states and the national state that was to come.[7] This move included a determined effort to bring primary and secondary education under central control in order to get it out of the hands of religious orders. The new constitutional government charged its

Ministry of Public Instruction with the task of building a secularized and uniform state system.[8] A major education act in the 1850s made state educational officers responsible for primary and secondary education in each of the provinces of Piedmont. Although these field officers had to work with provincial boards, the bureaucratic source of their power steadily strengthened.[9] Held responsible for seeing that municipalities complied with standards set by the state, they became active officers of the line, carrying the fight against local and religious control.

As for the state universities, they were put under the direct supervision of the Ministry of Public Instruction situated in Turin. Here was the model of control that Piedmont, as the model constitutional state for the rest of Italy, was to bring to the governing of education. The administrative pattern of Piedmont, in which the public university was placed directly under a ministry, was carried to the national level in the Casati Education Act of 1859, which sought to regulate all levels of education. The universities were formally nationalized at that time. Yet, in practice, a high degree of university autonomy prevailed. A strong move toward a unified system did not take place until the 1920s.[10]

In the half-century of nation-building between the completion of national unification in 1870 and the coming to power of Mussolini in the early 1920s, the administrative logic of the separate states was transferred to the national level and there greatly extended and elaborated. The Liberals who brought the Italian government into being and were so long in power were strongly committed to administrative centralization. If the new state were to become a nation, it would have to overcome local loyalties and traditions that had been entrenched for centuries. It would somehow have to establish a unitary legitimacy across the seemingly unbridgeable differences between Naples and Milan, Sicily and Piedmont. Any major decentralization of decision-making from the center to lower units of government could be disruptive: "Administrative centralism [was] a necessary phase of the country's development," since "the only way to political unity lay in a national administration immune to the dangers of regionalism."[11]

The heads of the new democratic state feared that dissident groups would split the nation if given a chance. The Catholic church made it clear it would do so, withholding support of the new government for decades; the peasants of the south were clearly outsiders and their discontent could lead to revolution; and the workers of the north, socially distant from the elite, were also not closely identified with the new state. With so many alienated groups, federalism would have been a great danger. The better way, and perhaps the only way, was to have as much administration as possible in Rome, in the hands of the vigorous minority that had made the nation, and then to deploy dependable agents into the field.

Connected to the fear of dissident forces was a distrust of the capacity of the masses to participate effectively. The Liberals were elitist democrats. They believed in parliament, periodic elections, and the rest of the formal machinery of the democratic state; but they restricted sharply who could elect and who could legislate.[12] They did not worry about responsiveness to the public or about swift decision-making.[13] They sought to construct a unifying state machinery whose good work would bring to the state credibility in the eyes of other nations and eventual legitimacy within all of the peninsula. The centralizing of power was not only a way of struggling simultaneously against the church, other countries, and the fragmenting pluralism of the various regions and strata but also a way to let the responsible few rule the nation while tutoring the masses for possible later participation.

Thus there were many strong impulses in the new nation to strengthen national central administration at the expense of local and provincial government. Here there were to be no German *Länder* or American states, nor even strong prefects, it turned out, to supervise the provision of education and other public services. Centralization and concentration in *administration* became the norm, expressed in the functioning of national ministries and offices that in time turned central administration from its virtues to its vices. By the turn of the century, just thirty years after the full unification, prime ministers of the government were noting the need for reform of the administrative structure on the grounds that centralization and concentration were stifling initiative in the field and causing everything to bog down in details.[14] And the practice of swelling the government offices to ungainly size as a means of reducing intellectual unemployment, as well as serving bureau aggrandizement, was by then already firmly institutionalized. In the short period from 1904 to 1907, the Italian legislature enacted fifty-five laws that enlarged various strata of government workers—a process known as *organico-mania.* [15]

The Fascist period that began in 1922 and lasted for two decades carried centralization and concentration in the Italian government to new heights, greatly enlarging its bureaucratic aspects. Not only were the basic ministries expanded in number and size, but ad hoc public agencies were created at a rapid rate, to the point where more than 250 central authorities were carrying out activities throughout the country. [16] These bureaus, each in its own sphere, centralized in Rome the authority to hire personnel down to the lowest grades and to disburse funds above very limited amounts. [17] Local government, and local branches of the central government, grew weaker as the Fascists concentrated political authority. But the Fascist regime of Mussolini failed to maintain tight coordination within the center, allowing considerable administrative authority to be exercised by the numerous bureaus. The central bureaucracy in Italy had become a fourth branch of government, and "democratic politics was replaced by bureaucratic politics." [18]

Of special interest for our purpose is how little the postwar government, in the years between 1945 and 1970, pulled back from the peak of centralization and concentration reached in the Fascist period. Parties in power in Rome preferred that power stay in Rome; the Left, out of power, was willing to decentralize power and hence to point to all the negative aspects of control from Rome. In the years immediately after the war, the Center and the Right were soon opting for a reconstruction of the pre-Fascist centralized state. De Gasperi, backed by the Allies and with the support of his own Christian Democrats, the Liberals, and factions to the right, pledged himself to this effort. [19] As the Communists and Socialists emerged as the dominant political force in the regions of Tuscany, Umbria, and Emilia-Romagna, any move toward regionalization of authority posed the possibility of a Red Belt across north-central Italy. Hence the Christian Democrats were all the more in favor of retaining power in Rome. There was no lack of criticism of centralization; indeed criticism was everywhere, and, in reaction to the excessive controls of the Fascist regime, a provision for decentralization of legislative and administrative power to regional governments was written into the new Italian constitution of 1948. But that provision remained largely unimplemented through the 1950s and the 1960s, not receiving application across the nation until a regional decentralization law was enacted in 1970.

Balkanized Administration

Along with centralization and concentration, Italian public administration has also shown a marked tendency for authority to be split among quasi-autonomous agencies of the center. In structural terms, vertical lines of authority have been growing stronger around specific jurisdictions, while lateral linkage has been weakening both at the top and at points down the line, with neither the national prime minister nor the area prefect nor the town mayor able to coordinate the agencies. This tendency was evident in the early Liberal state, but the Italian government of the early decades was much simpler in structure. A strong national leader, such as Giolitti, could still reach effectively across the national agencies in the early 1900s, when there were only eight or nine ministries and 100,000 state civil servants.[20] Even so, the critics who thought centralization a major defect at the turn of the century were also pointing to disconnected action of various central offices as a weakness of Italian public administration. There was already "a trend toward complete autonomy of the various state field services," with exclusive channels of communication and hierarchical dependence.[21] The Fascist government, though greatly enlarging governmental authority, dispersed it in a plethora of agencies, carrying bureau autonomy to new heights. The structure of government became Byzantine, loaded with twilight zones within which special agencies acted along the lines of their separate functions, with little coordination.

After World War II, the De Gasperi government, faced with many difficult tasks in restoring and strengthening the nation, further expanded the administrative machinery, throwing new burdens on the traditional services and creating new agencies and services that were to operate outside the main framework of state administration. Thus, the proliferation of agencies continued, and coordination became even more a seemingly unsolvable problem.

The Italian style of public administration is not unknown elsewhere, in federal as well as in unitary governmental structures. In the United States, federal agencies have been growing ever stronger as they have been growing ever more numerous. To enhance autonomy, many bureaus have been deliberately isolated from central executive control. At the same time, state and local governments in the United States have grown weaker in relation to the federal level and have been increasingly unable to coordinate effectively at their own levels. Within the central administration that grows ever stronger major bureaucracies have developed a center-to-field capacity to reach constituencies, and, in so doing, to develop supportive interest groups. Experts and clients develop mutual self-interest around a vertical line of administration. There is no equally strong dynamic in the service of lateral linkage. One participant-observer of American government has argued that its so-called cooperative federalism has become a cooperative feudalism—a "federalism of balkanized bureaucracies, segmented legislative committees, and fragmented program administration."[22] In this view, even *federal* organization is in danger of succumbing to the power of "vertical functional autocracies" operating largely as "self-governing professional guilds."[23]

Italian public administration is an extreme case of this general phenomenon of balkanized bureaucracy. Developed in the framework of a unitary rather than federal state, the phenomenon has been little opposed by the countervailing power of regional and municipal government. It has been promoted by the long-standing belief of national ruling elites that lower levels of government could not be trusted to work effectively in the national interest.

The fear of local and provincial government has not remained as strong as it was in the early decades of the new nation, but as the fear subsided it was replaced by the self-interest of central bureaus in retaining power and administration at the center. What has become weak at the center in Italy is the ability to coordinate an ever more unwieldy aggregation of agencies, most of which have the need, the wish, and the capacity to reach to the grass roots of the nation. The result has been strong verticality in increasingly separated ministries and bureaus. In the words of one Italian observer:

> Every branch of the public administration, every public service, is today a feudal fief of a group of bureaucrats who

like the medieval barons give only a purely formal recognition to the sovereignty of the power that invested them with their fief. Each group of bureaucrats has its own sphere of influence in certain agencies or offices or corporations subsidized by, controlled by, or dependent on the government.[24]

Or, put more abstractly as a problem of coordination:

At the bureaucratic level, the lack of coordination is very high. . . . This same lack of coordination applies also, within both ordinary and special administration, to the relationship among the various organs, and again to the relationship of these with local government. The system suffers, in conclusion, from a very high degree of verticality.[25]

This is not to say that there are no lateral linkages among agencies. Budgets must be worked out between various agencies and the Ministry of the Budget (*Bilancio*). Some actions have to be decided across several bureaus (a process known as *concerto*) and hence require political exchanges among partner-bureaus. But it is widely acknowledged that the horizontal relationships are weak compared to the vertical.

Balkanization is thus a basic condition of Italian public administration, one long in the making and deeply entrenched. With departments and bureaus going their own ways, it is difficult to effect public policy in even those activities where accountability is clearly possible, let alone in the murky realm of higher education. The general fragmentation of the national bureaucracy, which we shall call balkanization of the first degree, is a first line of defense for the autonomy of the professor against the political acts of the state. The bureaucrat and the professor alike are shielded by centralized *administration* that, in high degree, is autonomous in relation to centralized *political control*.

The Administrative Culture

Centralization and concentration in structure have interacted with a belief that the public interest is best served by central-agency bureaucrats. And the balkanizing of control has interacted with a way of thinking that promotes the connection of specific agencies to specific external interest groups. In the dominant pattern described by Joseph La Palombara as *clientela*,[26] an administrative agency will come to accept an interest group as "the natural expression and representative of a given social sector which, in turn, constitutes the natural target or reference point for the activity of the administrative agency."[27] Administrators then perceive public administration as a business of serving or promoting outside interests. In a second pattern— *parentela*—outside groups develop, through a sense of political or cultural kinship, a diffuse connection to a political party: for example, Catholic Action with the Christian Democratic Party in Italy. *Parentela* relationships also influence the administrative agencies.[28] *Clientela* and *parentela* relationships vary in strength among Italian agencies, but they are sufficiently customary to help sustain an administrative value system that looks with favor upon specific linkages between bureaucratic experts and client groups.

These forms of special favor are not, however, unopposed in the value system of the civil service. Any governmental bureaucracy has some strain toward legal rationality, and, in its century of development, the Italian bureaucracy has institutionalized a concern for uniform application of detailed administrative rules. Public administrators in Italy have generally taken their university degrees in the field of law, and, as La Palombara concludes, "it would be difficult to overemphasize the importance of the orientation to rationality that grows out of the bureaucrat's education in jurisprudence."[29]

Beyond their socialization to law, administrators come under role mandates that are extremely legalistic. Italy, like France and Germany, has a dense legal system that bears heavily upon administration. Since so many legislative and executive enactments apply to the operation of governmental agencies, there is a large body of administrative law. In turn, there is a special sector of administrative courts that are supposed to protect the individual against wrongful administrative acts and, notably, to supervise and control the handling of public monies.[30]

Within this framework, the Italian civil servant is pressed to be legalistic, feeling the weight of the law as he fixes his signature to various papers. The logic of his situation *qua* pure administration puts first the question, "Is it legal?" rather than questions of accuracy and efficiency.[31] Thus, with socialization and work role both pressing for obedience to the written law, public administrators are not simply pushed and pulled by demands of interest groups: "What the groups request must conform to a minimum framework of rationality."[32] Within their separate pyramids, administrators must balance between their commitment to clients and their orientation to legally defensible action.

The balance can take different forms. One ideal way is to have the protection of the client-group become, over time, a part of bureaucratic precedent, so that to obey the rule is to protect the client.[33] We shall later observe this form and the special shape that it takes in Italian higher education. Also, the fulcrum of balance can shift according to the relative strength of the legal orientation and the effective pressure of the client group. The law is supposed to be faithfully and exactly applied. But, as elsewhere in modern states, a vast body of regulations entails contradictions in rules and conflicts in standards that in practice allow much discretionary behavior. Thus, a client-group possessing high status and independent power that also has high access to the bureaucracy—in short, a group that can effectively exert pressure —can substantially shift the balance-point of administrative action in the direction the group desires. Then the bureaucracy can be made relatively passive, or it can be induced to make favorable and friendly interpretations of the rules to a whole group of clients or to particular individuals.[34]

Having looked at the Italian government as an administrative setting for the governance of higher education, we have established certain terms of discussion which directly reflect that setting: centralization, concentration, balkanization, control by bureaucratic norm, and structured influence of relevant interest groups. The terms are such that they may be used in further research as dimensions for comparing the administrative environments of higher education in other countries. Here our purpose is to see how they obtain in the structure and practice of the Italian bureau whose jurisdiction includes all of the higher education of the country.

THE BUREAUCRATIC LINES IN HIGHER EDUCATION

The intent to centralize and concentrate authority has also characterized the higher education sector. Much like the French, the Italians have tried by means of national legislation and national administration to establish detailed policies and procedures that would cause a set of universities to operate as if they were parts of a single national entity. The Bonaparte conception of a single university with provincial parts, long the official definition in France in the nineteenth century, was applied for a while in the early nineteenth century to French-controlled parts of Italy. After unification, the intentions of the Liberal elite to build an effective national administration included, as we have indicated, the universities as well as the rest of education. The concept was the very opposite of the American scheme, where the control of education early became located in the states and the private sector, with little systematic influence from the national government.

The Italian approach also differed sharply from the definitions that emerged in Britain and Germany. The British structure, so much influenced by the historic autonomy of Oxford and Cambridge, has managed to combine national funding and national concern over educational policy with a high degree of university autonomy in allocating money internally, devising curricula, and hiring personnel. Using the University Grants Committee to mediate the government-university relationship, as the universities came increasingly under the support of the national purse, the British have made no attempt to establish a national personnel system, a national curriculum, or even a finely textured budget that would closely earmark expenditures.[35] The German structure has been one of public universities supported at the provincial level (the *Land* government), roughly analogous to individual state support of state universities in the United States, with neither a private sector nor national control.[36] Thus among the large industrialized Western nations of fifty million inhabitants or more, only the Italians and the French have sought to steer higher education by means of national bureaucracy in a legally unified system.

Levels of Organization

As in the case of any other activity, national administration in higher education entails relations between a central office and administrative and operating units in the field, with at least a rough semblance of bureaucratic hierarchy. In its bare skeleton, the vertical structure in Italy divides into four main levels. At the bottom is the chair, roughly analogous to the American department as the primary unit for the organizing of teaching, but with one person, the chairholding professor, clearly in charge. Assistants are arrayed under him. At this level also there is the institute, the primary unit for the organization of research, headed by a chairholding professor doubling as director and in a way that has closely fused the teaching and research units (see Chapter 3). The second major level is the faculty (*Facoltà*), headed by a dean (*Preside*), which is simply an assembly of a number of chairs and institutes within a particular professional field or set of related disciplines whose combined jurisdictions form a larger domain of teaching and research. The third level, of course, is the university (*Università*), administratively embracing a number of faculties and chaired by a rector (*Rettore*). These are the field units and operating levels of the national structure.

Above the university, the structure jumps directly to Rome. Not only are there no city or provincial levels of academic government, but there are no regional levels of national administration, such as the prefecture which appears in other bureaus in Italy and France or the *Academie* which appears in the French national system of higher education. The Italian university is directly connected to the national center. Thus, the fourth major level is Rome, where the structure contains the Division of Higher Education (*Direzione Generale Istruzione Universitaria*), headed by a director, within the huge Ministry of Public Instruction; and then the minister of education himself and the staff of his office. At the very top, the primary structure has an important lateral appendage in the form of the Superior Council (*Consiglio Superiore dell'Istruzione*), which is formally advisory to the minister and within which a major subsection concentrates on higher education. The council apparently existed at the very beginning of the Italian national system, transferred upward from the Piedmont government; Matthew Arnold remarked on its operations in his observations on the state of Italian education in the 1860s.[37] From the peak of the national educational bureaucracy, the formal lines of authority extend to the prime minister and his cabinet, of which the minister of education is a part; and to the parliament, composed of a Senate and a Chamber of Deputies, each of which has a major standing committee on education.

The Nationalized Sectors

These major levels of vertical organization connect in complicated ways that are not to be deduced from a simple mapping but will become somewhat clearer as we gradually unravel them and elaborate their meaning. However, the Italian formal system has strived for simplicity in the form of decision at the center on procedure that will hold throughout the system—essentially administration by national mandate. Bureaucratic lines of influence flow from the center to the field, from the ostensible top to the ostensible bottom, as means of establishing unity and uniformity. One line is financial, involving the distribution of money. An important second line is curricular, involving a unitary approach to degrees, programs of study, and student evaluation. The third and most important area of national administration centers on personnel, the ways in which professors and their assistants are selected and assigned to positions, rewarded financially, and given status. The personnel sector is so important because of the power, status, and autonomy that are generally granted to academic men on the Continent once their careers lead them into senior positions.

One other area of decision-making that is important in cross-national perspective can be quickly disposed of as traditionally nonproblematic in Italy: this is university admission. The universities have not had autonomy in selecting students, as in England and the United States, since selection is to the system as a whole. But neither has a group of gatekeepers at the center been in a position to decide who to admit each year, since selection to the system had been automatic upon completion of certain types of secondary schools. This form of admission, general to the Continent, has been so settled as a traditional right of the student that, until at least the late 1960s, neither bureaucrats nor professors in the higher education sector could touch it. It has been understood that professors at the secondary level, themselves part of the national system, would do the actual selecting.

Finance. Without going into great detail, we can point to two basic aspects of university finance in Italy: most money comes from the national treasury and it does not arrive at the doorstep of the university in a lump sum. The universities have had their own revenues from landholdings and accumulated endowments and, because of their old connection with city-states, have received monies from their own cities. But the returns from these sources have been a declining share of total income. As one would expect for national-system universities, the overwhelming proportion of university monies now comes from the national government—approximately 70 percent in the early 1960s. The second largest source, student tuition and fees, amounted to about 20 percent of current expenses.[38] Among the remaining miscellaneous sources, there are, for some institutions, monies from private parties and hence income at the operating level that is not processed through Rome. An institute, particularly in such professional fields as medicine and engineering, may do research on contract from major firms—and may even accept contributions without performing a service. Sometimes, institute directors can also maintain small discretionary funds from laboratory fees that they collect directly from students. But the great bulk of money across the system—and in many fields such as the humanities almost all the money—comes from national agencies.

Among the agencies involved, the Ministry of Public Instruction has the primary role in that it prepares a budget for the entire university system, negotiates it with the Treasury (*Ministero del Tesoro*) and the cabinet, and sees it through the legislature, where it is debated and modified by the education committees of the Senate and the Chamber of Deputies and voted upon by the two houses.[39] The education ministry also has primary influence in determining the funds for construction of university buildings, although to do this it must develop some lateral connection to another agency, the Ministry of Public Works (*Ministero dei Lavori Pubblici*), which supervises construction in the public domain. A second national agency with a direct interest in education, the National Research Council (*Consiglio Nazionale delle Ricerche*), has been growing in importance to the operating levels of the universities in recent years through contracts for research projects, annual allotments for approved research centers, and research grants. In actual handling of disbursements and accounting for expenditures, the universities are directly related to the Treasury. In all cases, the important offices are at the center: to lobby for the budget, one does not go to a prefect or a local statehouse but to Rome, and there usually to the huge Kafkaesque building, on Viale Trastevere in the most genuinely Roman quarter of the city, that houses the education ministry.

Lobbying can have only marginal utility, however, since the budget is characteristically inflexible, either from the standpoint of the central administration or from that of the individual university. Set annually, the budget is largely a summation of fixed expenses committed in national categories and routinely accounted for along categorical lines. Salaries, the most important item, are fixed by civil service appointment and related "salary coefficients." More than in autonomous universities, in a national-system university the position of a tenured professor or established assistant is a sunk cost, since civil service gives such good job protection. The same kind of rigidity in control of positions that autonomous universities face when their established departments become accustomed to a certain size occurs on a magnified scale in the Italian national network, between the center and the three operating levels of university, faculty, and chair-institute. It is not easy to slice and take away. Similarly for the expenses of supplies and the maintenance of machinery and physical plant, monies are tied down both by past commitments and by allocations in categories and subcategories of expenditures that extend across the nation. The regular way to alter the budget is through an increase or decrease in a category, applied across the entire system as a percentage of the allocation of the previous year. The momentum of the budget is considerable. [40]

Neither lump-sum financing nor explicit transferability of funds from one category to another is normally available to rectors, deans, and professors. Instead, different major and minor budget categories run vertically, like stakes, from Rome down into the academic ground, through the university level of administration, and often through the faculty level, to the level where the work of teaching and research occurs. Thus, in finance, the universities have little autonomy. The administrative concentration and political centralization that characterize Italian government generally are thus reflected in the ways of financing higher education.

Curriculum. Centralization and concentration have also been heavily reflected in decisions on fields of study, courses, and credits. For any university to give the *laurea*, the single degree traditionally available in Italy, it must obtain official recognition and permission from the Ministry of Public Instruction. The right to award the *laurea* in particular fields has also been centrally controlled. The national government has specified the fields and the university must obtain permission specialty by specialty. The government has also specified what courses are included in each field of study: first, as required courses that hold throughout the country, and, second, as optional courses that vary somewhat among the universities.[41]

The best indicator of the presence of a national curriculum in Italy is a national code, revised periodically, that officially specifies what is available in the system. Published by the Ministry of Public Instruction,[42] the code details in some four hundred pages the curriculum structure of the nation. It first lists all the fields of study in which the *laurea* is granted somewhere in the national system—about forty areas in the 1960s (for example, philosophy, chemistry, and economics)—with no mention of individual universities. Second, it shows the fields of study according to the type of faculty in which they are located; for example, eight different degrees in science can be awarded within the faculties of mathematical, physical, and natural sciences. This second national classification also has no mention of any of the universities by name. A third long section specifies, for each field of study, its length (usually four or five years); its entrance requirements in terms of a diploma from certain kinds of secondary schools; its required courses (*insegnamenti fondamentali*); basic optional courses (*insegnamenti complementari*) that should be available anywhere that the field is given; and finally some additional optional courses that have been arranged by the individual universities, specifying by university where these options are found.

This official national document (in a midsixties edition) showed that the field of law had a four-year curriculum, required a diploma from a classical or scientific secondary school, contained eighteen required courses, twenty-three optional courses, and seventy-five additional options introduced by various universities, and required the student to take and pass examinations in all the required courses and in at least three of the complementary ones in order to qualify for the final examination for the degree. For political science, the code showed that a student anywhere in the country had to pass seventeen required courses and at least four others from among eleven nationally specified options and eighty-five university-specified ones. The universities had accumulated a large number of their own options, but the national regulations forced students everywhere to concentrate on the required courses that were system-wide: eighteen required courses to three options in law; seventeen required to four options in political science; twenty-four required to three options in medicine; and ten required to three options in foreign languages and literature. This ministerial publication concluded with a fifty-page appendix reporting in detail all the laws, royal decrees, and presidential decrees, from 1935 to date, that have established and modified the national curriculum.

The Ministry of Public Instruction also maintains a second, smaller code (100 pages) that breaks down the national curriculum by university and faculty,[43] a handy document for determining what faculties exist at each university and what fields of study are approved for each faculty. Here, the basic curricular structure of the system is exhibited in one large-page foldout: some forty rows list the degrees available in Italy (for example, *laurea* in *scienze politiche*, *laurea* in *architettura*) and about forty columns list the recognized universities and minor schools, including the "free" or private institutions; all the places giving a particular degree and all the degrees available at a particular university are shown in this tabular listing. Any fields and places not on this list are unrecognized by the central government—the only body that can offer accreditation—and are outside the system. Anything on the list is officially approved and guaranteed as acceptable for a degree awarded by the system.

The high specificity of this national curricular structure dates from the Fascist period. All through the Liberal period, that is, up to the 1920s, the universities had autonomy in determining curriculum. Many attempts were made from the very beginning of the Italian national system to instill more order from the center, right down to suppressing or starving peripheral universities in order to strengthen central ones, as well as allocating fields of study. But all such efforts were beaten back by interests devoted to the welfare of the peripheral institutions, from professors to shopkeepers.[44] Then, in 1923, the philosopher Giovanni Gentile, disciple of Benedetto Croce and minister of education in the early Fascist government, introduced standard requirements for degrees in different fields as part of an attempt to bring greater order into the state-supported and nominally state-controlled system and to raise standards in the universities.[45] Gentile wanted to maintain considerable university autonomy; the imposing German model of freedom of professors in research and teaching was evidently much in mind. But he also had some overriding concerns: Italian universities had drifted away from the fundamentals of philosophical study; the life of the student was outrageously soft, noted abroad as well as at home; the autonomy of the professors had led to excessive specialization, duplication, and self-indulgence; and there were too many universities turning out too many students.[46]

The power of the ministry of education under a dictatorship provided more room for change than had been available since the Casati laws in the earliest years of unification. Seizing the opportunity, Gentile gave administrative teeth to the long-standing but unfulfilled aspiration to have a national system. From that time, there was precedent and machinery at the center to intervene throughout the set of universities in the name of national standards. Later Fascist ministers of education, between 1935 and 1938, fully standardized the curriculum, as exhibited in the tables of study (*ordine degli studi*) described above.[47] The intent to make a national system had evolved from a general objective and a loose framework to national codes that formally united the offerings of all universities.

After World War II, the university system did not roll back these national regulations. The curriculum structure put together under the Fascists was retained, with the national catalogue reporting faithfully in every edition that it was rooted in the decrees of the late 1930s. In the three decades (1938–68) that followed the master decree, the grand list of fields of study grew only from thirty-seven to forty-five, an indication of the stability of the national structure. Through this curriculum control the Italian government has sought to guarantee parity among course offerings and degrees. As in France, the degree is understood to be a national degree awarded by the national system and not a degree of the individual university.

Once the national curriculum was institutionalized, it became exceedingly difficult for a professor or a faculty or a university to change the basic course of study in any field. In all cases, the ministry had to approve, because what was being changed was part of a nationally certified curriculum. For courses listed as optional and varying among the universities, some flexibility could be maintained, with even yearly changes. But the procedure was cumbersome: the request by a professor to introduce or retitle an elective course had to be approved by the *Facoltà* in which it originated, then by the university as a whole, and then by the ministry, including specifically the Superior Council; then the approval had to be transmitted back down the line. The request could be denied at any point, or simply fail to complete the circuit by bogging down somewhere—and having proposals bog down is a common way of denying them without formal action. An analogous situation in the United States would be if the introduction of a new course desired by a professor of physics at the University of Montana had to be processed through the several levels of that university and then sent on to a bureau in the Office of Education in Washington, D.C., there to be considered by a national advisory council as well as bureau officials and given an official signature of approval. In Italy, even a routine request for a new course required a decree of the president of the nation (*Decreto del Presidente della Repubblica*) before the course could, as an elective, be credited toward the degree.

The real difficulties of curricular change centered in the required fundamental courses in each field of study, since any change affects all universities. The required courses have been the cement of the unitary approach, the ostensible guarantees of uniformity, the intended reality of the rhetoric that to study law in one place is, in the eyes of the nation, equal to studying law in another. Since they are the centerpieces of the curriculum within each faculty, these courses have been part of the power base of the professors who teach and control them. Therefore, locally and nationally, a change in a required course has been a critical rather than a routine decision—one that has been closely guarded in the channels of review. Such channels have included not only bureau officials in the ministry committed to a national view but also, importantly, the Superior Council, composed of prestigious professors from the commanding heights of the strongest well-established disciplines. A change in the basic courses in law at the University of Turin was not possible without major debate around the issue of whether the change was desirable in all law faculties of the country and without a mustering of votes in the Superior Council as well as approval by the minister of education. The many obstacles in the structure of approval and system-wide implementation have ensured infrequent alterations and a stable national core curriculum. It was not until the 1970s that reforms began to change this national form of curricular control.

The national-system structure in Italy has also mandated that all courses be passed by examination, with the professor in charge of a course examining in the subject during examination periods common across the nation. The academic year, stretching from November to November, traditionally contained three "calls" for examination, scheduled for June, October, and February (although in recent years the calls have been expanded to cover several months each). Students were entitled to try the examinations twice a year. Until recently, if they did not pass in the normal length of time, they became counted as "out-of-course"— *fuori corso*—but retained in most fields the crucial right to take the examinations.[48] In several faculties (medicine, science, and engineering), the student prerogative to hold on for four years or more has been undermined by a requirement of passing examinations in certain courses within the first two years. This early barrier caused some failures in these fields to flow to "easier" faculties, especially teaching—an instance of the oldest, most classic form of the "cooling-out" function in higher education, namely, the institutionalized transfer of students from hard to soft disciplines, whereby the initial aspirations of students are transformed into acceptable second choices.[49]

Nearly all courses in the Italian curriculum have been seven months in length, extending from November to May. The compulsory ones have large enrollments and are supposed to have "official professors" in charge, which meant traditionally that they were under the direction of chairholding professors.[50] During the hectic examination periods, the professor and his assistants face not only those in the current class who elect to be examined but all those who failed in previous years and are back for another try. The examinations, which are mainly oral, have varied length, customarily extending for a half-hour to an hour but, under pressure of numbers in recent years, sometimes lasting as little as five to ten minutes.

The students must pass between sixteen and thirty-five examinations in four to six years, depending on his field of study. The average has been about twenty-two to twenty-three exams in four years, with about three-quarters in required courses. Thus, in a typical year, the student attempts five or six examinations: he signs up for the related course subjects in November, getting on the books so that when the official call for an exam period is made he has the right to be examined in those subjects. In the following months the student does not, for most courses, actually need to attend lectures or otherwise participate. He is free to prepare for the examination as he deems best, which may mean coming to listen to lectures, or only following the readings, or getting a tutor, or learning by discussion from friends, or taking a chance on passing the examination with little or no preparation. The only behavior that has really counted, the prime academic hurdle, has been the oral examination. There the student may encounter the professor himself. But as examination loads of professors have grown, students increasingly have faced examination by assistants, with official certification by the remote professor. The degree of contact between student and professor has varied depending on whether they are in crowded or uncrowded universities, that is, essentially the large, central places and the small, peripheral ones. It has also varied by discipline; the student in such well-structured, scientific fields as physics is more likely to see his professor during the year and be tested by him at the end than is the student in the more loosely structured and overcrowded fields found within "letters" or under the teacher-education faculty.

The final step to the *laurea*, the one and only important degree of the system, is a thesis written in the last year of study.

The orientation toward examinations in the whole Italian system of higher education is thus carried through under bureaucratic rules. But the rules only go so far and then stop: With all the emphasis on examinations, nowhere is it specified that they will be nationally prepared and nationally administered. There are no "external examinations," applied across the system and managed by officials, public or private, other than those who give the courses. Here, administration becomes radically decentralized. The university, the faculty, and specifically the chair have discretion in preparing the test; in effect, they have the authority to give specific content to a nationally prescribed form. It remains up to the individual professor to decide what examination questions to ask of whom and then to judge who has performed adequately and who has not. [51]

Thus, despite extensive nationalization of degrees and courses, and significant central control over changes in them, the means of judging student accomplishment have remained so autonomous as to vary from one professor to the next. There is, of course, no international rule or even common-sense logic that dictates that a nationalized curriculum must make every step uniform. Various values, including professorial freedom, must be served, and these are likely to cause compromise in national uniformity. Significantly, however, descriptions that tag the Italian system as nationally bureaucratic are misleading, even on the formal grounds of what is legally required. With all the many interlacing national rules on degrees, courses, and examinations, universalism remains decidedly incomplete. In this important sector of decision-making, bureaucratic vertical control does not run all the way down into the education ground.

Personnel. Italian professors and their assistants are part of the national civil service. To be hired to teach at the University of Pisa or the University of Salerno is to be placed in a personnel category of the government, given rank by the government, and paid by the government. Hence the system contains procedures for selection to categories and rules that establish status and salary.[52]

Selection. The procedures for appointing assistants and professors are specified in national law for uniform administration throughout the system. The most important decisions are reserved for central bodies, and the basic mechanism for these decisions is a national competition (*concorso*) convened by the Ministry of Public Instruction.

Starting at the bottom, the lowest of the low have been unpaid assistants. The "voluntary assistant" (*assistente volontario*) simply made his labor available to a professor, without going through a competitive procedure, as a way of getting started on an academic career after receiving the *laurea*. Although not on civil service lists, these lower assistants—often referred to as *precari*—were recognized in national law.[53] In fact, their existence was *de*-recognized by national law in the late 1960s, in an effort to reduce unpaid labor in university institutes. But professors usually need additional labor beyond the restricted supply of paid assistants, and aspiring young academics who are not selected for a paid position have an interest in making themselves available in auxiliary capacities. Also, in professional fields, particularly medicine, outside practitioners have an interest in possessing a university connection, and even a nominal position of assistant is a valuable addition to one's professional shingle. In one guise or another, such assistants have existed and will continue to exist: at the end of the 1960s, the number *officially* reported for all of Italy was nearly 18,000, compared to about 8,500 of the more solidly based assistants.[54]

There are some additional low-level assistants who are on small stipends, but the senior category among assistants, the coveted status in the early career, is that of *assistente ordinario*, who is a civil servant, paid by the state, and has tenure at this level. The overall number and general placement of these positions is centrally controlled: such jobs cannot be created by the individual university or faculty out of any free funds that it might hold. Here the filling of vacancies is authorized by the ministry usually in answer to a request initiated by a professor and approved by his own faculty. The requested position will be in relation to a particular professor and becomes embedded in his institute; however, a faculty can reassign these lower positions upon their becoming vacant.

The filling of these tenured slots comes formally through a public competition. The competitions are authorized by the minister of public instruction, publicized in a *Bullettino Ufficiale* of the ministry, and otherwise treated generally as part of the national personnel system.[55] But at this still low level of rank, the local units of administration have primacy of influence. The system formally places the *concorso* in the hands of the *Rettore* of the university where the vacancy exists; the professor who will be in charge of the assistant will have a particular person already in mind, commonly from within his own institute; the rector establishes a local selection committee, with the "official professor" in charge; and this local procedure leads to a nomination that goes to the ministry for formal approval, an announcement in an official report, and placement on the career civil service list.[56] Basically, all categories of assistants are handled locally; the center's function is largely that of routine processing. That processing is important for the newly tenured assistants, of course, since the assumption of a civil service position entails the assignment of a salary coefficient and the beginning of determination of subsequent salary by time in grade.

The tenured assistant and the tenured professor have been the primary positions in the rank structure. Between them there developed an untenured category of *professori incaricati.* The *incaricato* has been considered nearer to the full professorship than is the assistant: he is recognized as being responsible for courses, a privilege officially denied assistants, and he has a higher initial salary. But he was, until the reforms of the early 1970s, untenured, on short-term appointment with fixed salary, and thus hardly secure. He too has been largely selected locally, by the *Facoltà* in which the vacancy is lodged. The *incaricato* position is an important step in the academic career, since it gives its occupant certain duties—including teaching—on a par with those of the professor. Thus, more generally, the position is a waiting room for the top vacancies.

As junior faculty members attempted in the past to make their way through the various levels, they also had to meet another requirement. They had to obtain official recognition of the right to teach in the national system—the *libera docenza*. One could not apply for this right until five years after the *laurea*; one could not become full professor without it. To pass this requirement, it was necessary, in effect, to enter a national competition, that is, to submit one's application, backed by scholarly papers, to a national commission composed of full professors. Here the formal locus of decision shifted to the national level: the most advanced license of the academic world—similar to the *habilitation* in Germany—could not be awarded by the local faculty or university (or by the province, as in Germany). Neither *assistenti* nor *incaricati* had to have the *libera docenza*, but it could add salary increments and sooner or later it was a necessary step.

The serious business of the entire system has been the creating and filling of professorial chairs. Even in the relatively straightforward administrative framework set forth in this chapter, the business of chairs, and particularly the creation of new chairs, is enormously complicated. An American can begin to sense why by thinking of the chair as somewhat analogous to the department and then imagining that the creating of departments in American universities and the filling of a permanent chairmanship in each one would entail system-wide processes centered in the Office of Education in Washington.

The official process for the creation of new chairs commonly begins at the local level in the form of a request by the faculty, through the university, to the ministry for the creation of a chair in a particular discipline within the faculty. The matter is

discussed at the center and must there be approved by the
Superior Council and the minister. Then, to fill the chair, a
national public competition, a *concorso*, must be called. To
handle the *concorso*, an ad hoc national committee is formed for
the sole purpose of filling the one post. That committee meets not
at the initiating university but at the national center, and is
composed not of members of the one university but of chairholding professors, always five in number, drawn from various places
in the system. After public announcement in the official ministerial bulletin, the committee receives applications, examines, and
decides on the best qualified. Since the matter is taken to be so
important, it is not lacking in rules: five pages of regulations in a
compilation of university law are devoted to rules regarding the
competition, particularly the assembling of the "commission"
that administers the competition. [57] Legal and bureaucratic edicts
have ensured that the selection of a professor for a new position
receives deliberation across the system and at the center.

Chairs also become available by falling vacant. The national
pool of open chairs at any one time consists of previously
constituted and allotted chairs, as well as the newly established
ones. Vacant chairs are fixed in specific faculties: they do not
revert to the university as a whole, nor to the central ministry, for
reallocation. The faculty can fill the vacancy by asking for a
competition, the same mechanism used in filling newly created
chairs. But it can also cover the opening by calling a chairholder
from some other place. Thus, transfer is possible, and it has
often been used by prestigious faculties in central universities.
The peripheral places are likely to need a competition in which a
new professor is appointed, since they are not generally desirable
places to which to transfer.

Around vacant chairs, faculties, on formal grounds alone,
build power in the selection process. The power is based first in
rights to chairs (*posti di ruolo*) once they have been assigned.
Holding such rights means that a faculty has a portfolio of chairs:
when one or more become vacant, the faculty can decide when
they should be filled, an additional source of power, and then,
what is most important, whether to fill by transfer or new
competition. The calling of a person who is already a chairholder
at another place maximizes local power, because in that instance
the devices that operate at the administrative center, in the form
of the national competition, are not brought into play.

However, no one becomes a chairholder without having entered a specific national competition. In short, access to the national pool of chairs, in any one discipline and in all disciplines taken together, is controlled by the center. In addition, the formal allocation of selection powers is made by the center. Who has which rights is prescribed for all the universities in one national set of rules. The rules can be rewritten only at the center through legislative enactment and ministerial decree.

The basic effects of bureaucratic centralism on the nature of selection in a set of universities place Italy toward one extreme in a continuum of formal selection systems. In the United States, a professor at the University of Wisconsin is appointed by faculty, administration, and trustees at that university; a Harvard professor is appointed by Harvard personnel alone. The national government is involved neither in establishing positions nor in appointing a specific individual. In Great Britain, the University of Leeds selects its own, as does Oxford. Neither needs to seek the approval of London on the creation of position or on actual appointment, although the national government provides the basic finance for both institutions, and the University Grants Committee makes allocations to the universities within broad categories. In Germany, the University of Heidelberg, like other German universities, recommends ranked candidates to its *Land* ministry of education, and hence government at the state level enters the processes of personnel selection—but not the central government. In France, the situation is close to that found in Italy: the national system must create the opening and a national committee must pass on the qualifications of candidates put forward by the individual university. But at least the initial search and screening seems to be reserved to the appropriate faculty within the university. Finally, in Italy, positions are created and allocated by the center; men and women are selected for a national pool by a central commission that operates in the name of the entire network of universities; and selection to a specific post is either by transfer from within the national pool or by means of examination by national commission. Centrally constituted bodies and centrally operated mechanisms thus influence personnel selection somewhat more in Italy than they do in France and considerably more than in Germany, Great Britain, and the United States.

The Italian national system moves personnel allocation toward the single mold of administered state monopoly and largely eliminates the formal bargaining and open competition that play some part in the allocation of personnel in national systems that are formally pluralistic. The individual Italian university has weak tools with which to compete openly for a desired academic. It is constrained by mechanisms that provide for a national pool and often offer a university a choice only among several candidates selected by a central committee. Some competition ensues, since the calling of men from other places to fill chairs establishes some interuniversity mobility and several places may desire a particular individual. But what one university has to offer that is different from others is usually a fixed characteristic—its geographic location and historic name—rather than a manipulable feature such as higher salary. From the side of the individual, the candidate cannot openly bargain among the universities that desire his services, as can his counterpart in Germany, who can maneuver among the eleven *Länder* ministries of education which formally negotiate with those who have been nominated by their own universities.[58] The Italian formal system is meant to restrain selective flows of academics so that they will not bunch together in distinctive clusters, causing institutions to be diverse in style and emphasis. Instead, the systemwide machinery has pressed toward uniform allocation by removing important aspects of recruitment and selection from local hands.

But the striving for national system has had hidden effects that are the opposite of uniformity controlled from the top. If individual universities do not have formal independence in selection, and individual candidates and incumbent professors have little genuine bargaining power in maneuvering among the universities, then voluntary movement in the system is difficult. The encompassing system discourages the "exit decision,"[59] the voluntary decision to leave one place and enter another that allows personnel to be independently mobile in the search for better opportunity—the decision personified, in the extreme, by the itinerant cosmopolitan of the American academic scene. Nevertheless, individuals seek to better themselves, especially when they think they might move into such a cherished position as that of a chairholding professor in a European system; if the system does not allow for open voluntary flow, the search for individual betterment is bound to move in other directions. One obvious direction is to attempt to be mobile through such unofficial means as friendship, patronage, and bargaining. Another means is to dig in locally, there to exercise an increasingly powerful voice. In the Italian personnel structure, a chair-holding professor is indirectly encouraged to maximize bargaining power around the place where his roots are permanently sunk. As we will see in detail, both the pattern of mobility through ties of patronage and that of local power enlargement make an ostensibly bureaucratic system more political by encouraging self-interest to become attached to essentially political mechanisms.

In sum, the ironic possibility exists that the effort to effect bureaucratic centralism in national systems of higher education may itself encourage its opposite, strengthening the tendencies that it purportedly should overcome. In Italy, as we shall see, that possibility has been realized.

Civil Service Seniority. One way in which the Italian national system does indeed anchor its key personnel, the full professors, in centrally controlled organization is by means of civil service status, and, specifically, by seniority within national ranks. As in many other branches of government employment in many governments—for example, the American military—the ranking is person by person. It has been made public in a document issued by the Ministry of Public Instruction and devoted solely to this purpose.[60] Extending to more than six hundred pages, this book of rank contains three major lists: an integrated national seniority list; seniority lists for individual faculties, reported university by university; and, less important, a list of professors grouped according to teaching specialty. (An alphabetical index of names at the end typically gives three page references for each professor; one's friends and enemies can thus be quickly located.)

The integrated national seniority list is broken down into five salary classes, each with a specified salary coefficient, of which the top four have been for the *professori ordinari* and the bottom one for a new rank of *professori straordinari*, in effect another waiting room for those soon to become *ordinario*. There has been virtually automatic ascent from the fifth to the fourth category, and guaranteed progression in seniority sets with appointment to *ordinario* and placement in the fourth *classe di stipendio*. After five years, the professor moves to the third class, after four more

years into the second, and after another four is assigned to the
top bracket—making thirteen years between entry to the professorship and placement in the top pay bracket, if everything moves
on schedule. Within each bracket, professors are listed by
seniority. Thus, in 1968, the ranking professor in all of Italy in
civil service seniority, Professor Gioacchino Scaduto of the
University of Palermo, appeared as the first-line item in the
highest salary class. His line also reported that he was born on
June 3, 1898, in Agrigento, and that he has three civil service
dates: he was first admitted to the general list on February 2,
1923; he ascended to the full professorship on September 18,
1924, a year and a half later; and he was included in the present
top bracket when the existing set of categories replaced a previous
scheme on April 16, 1958. Similar information was provided on
each professor in the 1968 edition, for 1,036 ranked in the first
class, 377 in the second, 502 in the third, 115 in the fourth, and
755 in the fifth, totaling 2,785 who were rank-ordered at the time
in the full national list.

Such precise placement on a grand list naturally has involved
ways of making fine distinctions, as when several professors have
been assigned to the same salary category on the same date, and
additional criteria are needed to rank them. Seniority credit has
been awarded for previous service within or without the state
system: for example, teaching in a secondary school or at a
foreign university may be given a credit as precise as "six years,
nine months, and two days."[61]

The second part of the volume has been equally careful in both
placing each professor in a category and in ranking him within it.
Persons are shown by the faculty to which they belong, with the
faculties grouped under the universities of which they are a part.
Thus each faculty has its own seniority list. Sometimes a list has
numbered rows with no names (indicating vacant positions),
sometimes only a single professor, sometimes more than fifty, as
in the Faculty of Letters and Philosophy at the University of
Rome. Included are the faculties of the so-called free or nonstate
universities. As part of the price of admission to recognized
university status, the nonstate universities come under the blanket
of civil service logic on seniority status.

No matter how lightly or heavily used by various individuals
and groups in Italy, such lists, seen in comparative perspective,

dramatize fundamental formal features of a national system. Strange customs, indeed, to the eyes of Americans, they underscore the fact that the professor in an Italian state university holds his position by virtue of appointment by a national system and also that his progression in salary and official standing is determined by the rules and administration of that system. The ministerial documents also make clear that, although the free universities are not strictly a part of Italian public administration, they have to some extent been absorbed into state-established modes and categories. Such lists leave us with no doubt that the Italian state has attempted to make a unitary national system through transforming university personnel matters into civil service procedure.

The Means of National Control

With so many rules and procedures applied to all universities, the Italian academic can hardly escape knowing that he is part of a national system. Further, whatever his personal inclination to conform or to deviate, he is likely to be aware that the center of the system possesses certain means of control. One such means, impersonal in its general form, is national law; a second is a class of officials who act at the universities as arms of the center, with responsibility for enforcing certain rules.

National law. The present body of law concerning higher education, as noted earlier, had its roots in the efforts during the Fascist period to introduce order and uniformity: first, by a general set of university regulations promulgated in 1924 by Gentile; next, by a thorough and detailed overhaul by a later Fascist minister of education in 1933–34, which established a single, unified set of rules (*testo unico*) for the system; and by some additions enunciated in 1938.[62] In each year since 1945, some changes or additions have been made,[63] usually minor in nature though occasionally important, as in the case of the laws passed in 1958 and 1962 that regularized the pay of professors on the seniority scale.[64] The volume that attempts to bring all university legislation together within one set of covers has various indices that themselves run to eight hundred items and twenty pages to guide readers through a thousand pages of legally enacted specifications.[65] This complex body of national university law is backed by the specialized courts set aside in the Italian judiciary to supervise public administration. As in the other sectors of government, administrators understand that policy is *in* the law; their task is to see that decisions hew to the law.

It is in the financial matters of the university that the control of law is most put to work. As in other countries, Italy tends to make a rough division between business and academic matters. The academic side—selecting teachers, establishing courses, and organizing teaching and research—permits local discretion. But the business side is understood as a serious matter of the state. Civil servants in the education and financial ministries in Rome busy themselves in deciding on legally correct authorization of expenditures and a legally correct accounting for disbursements. And the consequences of an improper expenditure of funds are far more severe than those attending mistakes in academic matters—for example, improperly changing a course listing or substituting the name of one person for another in a teaching assignment.

Administrative directors. The bearing of administrative law is reflected in the work of the second primary means of national control, the class of administrators at the universities who are field agents of the national government. Rectors and deans who are considered responsible for "the education side" of university affairs, do not fall in this category (they are "peculiar" officials, considerably creatures of the local scene, and we take up their special role later in this chapter). Each university has an administrative director (*Direttore Amministrativo*) who, in bureaucratic terms, is regular rather than peculiar. A true civil servant, appointed by the center as a permanent administrator of the business side of the university, he is legally responsible for administratively correct action, especially in expenditures. Hence his self-interest dictates that he be knowledgeable about the national rules in order to apply them to local decisions. The longer he stays in his post, the more his expertise on correct action increases over that of amateur administrators and professors. And the larger the university, the greater the scale of university finance and business operations, the more does his post evolve from business secretary to business manager.

The administrative director's influence is enhanced by the necessity of interpreting national laws while attempting to apply them, deciding on which regulations to apply to which cases and in what way. The inconsistent rules and conflicting standards of large administrative systems give headaches to rule-obeying officials but they give influence to those who put the rules to work in favor of their own inclinations.[66] The great complexity of the written rules for running an Italian university widens the opportunity for the main field agents of the center to enhance their power over others on the local scene by active interpretation. But even a passive posture in attempting to follow the rule book can be an important source of influence, since the administrative director's signature of approval is necessary on the papers that must go forward to authorize expenditures and later to account for them. There is power in inaction or simple delay, especially when overload brings the excuse of overwork.

With the administrative director in the university serving as a regular line officer of the national bureaucracy, assisted locally by his own office of civil servants, vertical bureaucratic structure is the main tool of coordination across the nation in finance and accounting. Here local autonomy is minimal. And it is here that professors at the university, in order to have influence, must make their peace with bureaucrats. As a result, administrative directors are widely disliked and feared; they are discussed in hostile tones by professors and students alike either as petty bureaucrats oriented to routine handling of detailed and legalistic measures or as politicized bureaucrats who manipulate the rules to favor their friends and their politics. As field agents of the center, their power is independent of that which is generated in the chair of the professor and in the academic bodies that are locally constituted for the general direction of academic affairs. They constitute the chief means by which bureaucratic agencies of the center reach into the life of the Italian university. It is here that the vertical stake does run all the way from the very top in Rome straight down into the educational ground.

THE DOUBLE BALKAN
We earlier portrayed the administration of the Italian state as heavily balkanized, with functional autonomy expressed in a structure of quasi-independent administrative pyramids. We have now noted certain features of the university sector that are likely to cause it to behave administratively in a balkanized way. There is national organization alone, with budget and curriculum

nationally determined and all personnel hired, ranked, and paid by the civil service of the one ministry alone. There are unitary procedures that are highly specific and legally binding, and that are guarded in the field by administrators whose careers are entirely within this one bureaucracy. The autonomy from other sectors that is typical of balkanized administration definitely obtains. Internally, as well, there are elements of central control and down-the-line coordination—characteristics of a unitary pyramid. Especially in financial matters, with law and administrative directors at work, considerable vertical reach prevails.

But there is much else in university administration besides finance, and we need to reexamine the general university structure to determine the fate of pyramidal control in other matters. Is this an administrative domain where bosses are bosses from the top to the bottom, in a bureaucratic structure of superordinant and subordinant positions?

The university pyramid is composed from the top down of:
. the minister of public instruction in Rome
. the Division of Higher Education within the ministry, headed by a bureau chief and consisting of some nine or ten staff sections
. university rectors, serving as chief campus officers at the different universities, and the administrative directors, serving as chief business officers—a situation of dual authority in some matters
. deans of the faculties
. chairholding professors and institute directors
. several levels of nontenured professors and assistants below (here, to simplify, lumped together as one stratum)

These levels of authority and responsibility do indeed have the formal shape of a pyramid that is narrow at the top and very broad at the bottom. But the pyramid also has unusual features that decisively affect how it operates, even in strict formal terms, and give it a structure unlike that of normal public bureaucracies.

Deviations from the Bureaucratic Pyramid

The first striking feature is a definite break in the vertical chain of command. The rectors and deans, at the third and fourth levels, are not appointed from above, but are elected from below. The rector of a university is elected by chairholding professors of that particular university for a term of three years.[67] Renewal of term is possible only if a majority of professors remains so committed. The system functions as one of short-term rotation in which peers elevate one among themselves to the rectorship but can soon pull him back into the ranks. The same system holds for the deans of the faculties, who are elected by the chairholding professors of their particular faculties for three-year terms.[68] Having often consolidated power within a faculty, deans may stay longer in office than do rectors, but the principle still operates: they are elected from below or from within the group rather than appointed as bureaucratic officials. The center can influence these decisions, since it is wise to elect a man acceptable to central officials, but the local clusters of professors have the power to select.

The structure thus deviates from the logic of bureaucracy. In place of appointment by superiors *or* selection by impartial examination, there is election by peers or nominal subordinates. The formal integration of the overall pyramid is thereby considerably weakened. There cannot be a dependable chain of command stretching from the deans upward to the rectors and then upward to the national center, since the rectors and deans are responsible chiefly to their own colleagues and, if not to them, to themselves. The top can only weakly exert leverage at the middle, for the middle is first beholden to a lower stratum. Collegial authority takes over; it is expressed specifically in the principle of election from among peers and also in the form of strong collegial bodies: at the university level, the Academic Senate (*Senato Accademico*) and the Administrative Council (*Consiglio di Amministrazione*); and, within each faculty, the Faculty Council (*Consiglio di Facoltà*). These bodies, rather than the single officals, are considered by the teaching personnel to be the main loci of academic power at the respective levels; indeed, their considerable powers are spelled out in national law.[69] We return to their operation in Chapter 3.

The second striking feature is a concentration of high social status and high civil service rank at the level of the chairholding professor within the faculties. Italian professors are no mere fifth-level bureaucrats. In his classic study of Italian prefects, Robert C. Fried grouped full professors in the state universities along with the "highest officials in rank and salary of the Italian bureaucracy," placing them, along with a few other high-ranking offices, at a level in the public bureaucracy "outranked only by the First President of the Court of Cassation, the presidents of the Council of State and of the Court of Accounts, and a small group of ambassadors."[70] The high civil service rating of professors had apparently accrued to them as a status commensurate with the traditionally high prestige of professors in Italian society.

Like professors elsewhere, Italian academics are strongly attached to traditions that emphasize the autonomy of individual scholars and communities of scholars, definitions that allow academic men to resist the labels of employee, official, and clerk. These powerful self-concepts, together with high social status in the general society, would, in themselves, create a situation in which the professors would not be easily controlled. But their capacity to resist bureaucratic command does not depend simply on an attitude; it has been built into the bureaucratic structure in the form of superior civil service rating. The bureaucratic structure has accommodated men of power by assigning them bureaucratic status that is exceedingly high for their position in the vertical chain of command for higher education. The result is that a faculty or university of medium to large size is an astonishing concentration of "bureaucratic rank." Imagine having several dozen, or several hundred, top prefects side by side in a single field unit of national administration.

If collegial election breaks the vertical chain of command at the levels of rector and dean, and then, at the next level down, there is great concentration of high rank, it is not surprising that the pyramid logic is reasserted with a vengeance at that lower level. The chairholding professor is a permanent official—non-rotating, nonelected—who can control several levels of subordinates, while little control is exercised over him. For all within his own administrative domain, he appoints, rates, recommends for promotion, and dismisses. Overranked by normal bureaucratic standards, he has, strictly on formal grounds, power to spare.

In short, the structure is doubly balkanized. The entire higher education sphere is organizationally set off as a large quasi-autonomous administrative sector of a government department. This subgovernment in turn is formally truncated at the point where the center links to the field, and great rank and power are there reintroduced to control subdomains. The truncated pyramid is an *administrative* source of *local* authority, systematically enhancing power in the chair, with little provision for either horizontal or vertical coordination that would abridge that power. The result is an extremely balkanized structure at the operating levels of the national system, the opposite of what is denoted when one refers to Italian higher education as a case of bureaucratic centralism.

There is even more that is bureaucratically unusual. The administrative structure is so flat that it would strain any coordinating capacity, let alone that of amateur administrators who are voted in and out of office on quick rotation. With thirty universities, there are thirty sets of rectors and administrative directors in the first level of administration under the center. Within the major universities, there are some eight to twelve faculties. And, most important, within the large faculties, "under" the dean, there is often a large number of chairs. Given only the geographic dispersion and structural spread of the constituent units, it would take great determination and imagination to devise over a period of time the tools of administrative integration whereby officials at the center would control the rectors, the rectors would control the deans, and the deans would control the professors.

Thus, we observe a structure inclined toward low accountability: one that is flat in general shape, possessing clear breaks in the vertical line, and exhibiting concentrations of power in the lower field units. The numerous small pyramids topped by local chiefs are unlikely to be under the mandates of accountability that are normal in unitary pyramids. A national organization that is doubly balkanized will have weak enforcement of those bureaucratic rules that are left for someone in the local pyramids to observe.

Techniques of Integration

Any modern, complex organization has some impulses toward fragmentation, and large national services always contend with powerful forces that pull their lower officials in field locations along many different paths.[71] But for all such organizations there are a number of possible techniques of integration whereby the tendency to dissolve into an aggregate of separate entities can be overcome. Sorting the techniques into three types, there are devices that preform decisions, procedures for checking up on decisions, and ways to socialize officials into common values and norms so that they voluntarily conform and render dependable decisions.[72] The Italian higher education system is relatively strong in efforts to predetermine decision, as shown in the bureaucratic lines we have described in budget, curriculum, and personnel. Specific formal issuances spell out courses of action, authorizing what may be done, directing what must be done, and prohibiting what must not be done. The laws and rule books are plentiful and there is no end of directives from Rome. The Italian system is not lacking in such techniques of integration.

But the checking-up machinery is something else. If techniques of detecting deviation in decision-making are to work, an administrative system needs some combination of such procedures as regular reporting from below, inspection from above, sanctions against deviation, appeal channels for aggrieved workers and clients, and movement of personnel from one locale to another in order to break up local cliques and interrupt systematic falsifications. In the Italian system, there is little by way of detailed reporting on university-level, faculty-level, and chair-level decision-making. Most important, there is no inspection. In Italy, as in other national unitary educational systems, there are inspectors for the elementary and secondary schools, men who, as they travel from one school to the next, serve as the wandering eyes and ears of higher authorities. But the norms of academe and the general understanding of the special place and status of professors are reflected in the higher education sector in a no-inspection system. No agent of Rome comes stomping into the offices, lecture halls, and laboratories of the professors to see if their behavior conforms to the requirements of decisions made at the center. Not at least as regular procedure. The ministry can send out its own representatives as inspectors or special commissioners in the event of a gross irregularity, such as corruption that comes to light or open defiance of accepted rules. But in the normal flow of work, the men of the field units of this national administrative structure do not need to fear the inspector-general.

Similarly for the integrative efforts of socialization. The preparation to be a professor is not one of instilling a common point of view as administrative agents of a national organization. There is no unified training, and, even among on-the-job professors, specialization tends to lead to divergent rather than convergent thinking. Socialization tends to take place only within the many small pyramids composed by the individual professors and institutes, and chairholding power leads toward an understanding of the professor as ruler within his domain. The general tendency is contrary to a mentality of reflecting faithfully policies and procedures laid down by a central ministry.

The result of strong rule-setting efforts but weak checking-up and weak socialization is an elaborate scheme of formal rules with little or no enforcement and no absorption of a national point of view. The formal arrangements thus present a system in which rules are announced but not enforced, with no one particularly interested in obedience. There is thus the possibility that the formal system serves as a public face, a mask, behind which various personal adjustments are made. Who knows whether a dean or a professor obeys a national rule or not? Who is in a position to care and to bring authority to bear against deviation? Behind the formal rules, and considerably *because* of the nature of the means of integration, there may be particularistic definition of the content of the rules. Despite the large books of impersonal rules, authority may well be highly personalized.

Limits of Bureaucratic Control

Returning to our original problem of coordination of a national system, we can now formulate the Italian system of universities as follows.
1. A national agency has been created as a means of coordination, one that has followed the general logic of Italian public administration in possessing much autonomy from other public and private sectors.
2. The agency has taken on many aspects of a bureaucracy, particularly a large body of laws and rules that are supposed to be applied uniformly across the universities of the country.
3. The national organization cannot coordinate its many parts effectively in a bureaucratic manner, however, since internally it is severely balkanized and possesses only weak techniques of integration. With its internal fragmentation of control, the organization takes on some qualities of a federation. Depending on how power is exercised among the parts, there may even appear some qualities of coalition among highly independent estates or other characteristics of loosely joined sets of organized groups. [73]
4. The balkanized units are clusters within which one person has

strong authority over all others. Connected to the historical development of universities as a form of guild organization, the local clusters exhibit a guild characteristic in the control of a high-status master over a domain of work. Balkanization of national organization may be viewed as an accommodation of bureaucratic overstructure to guild understructure, one that has helped strengthen the hegemony of the chair professor over a body of subordinates.

5. Although bureaucratic structure cannot coordinate, the visibility of its offices and procedures leads many insiders and outsiders alike to think there is an administratively coordinated system. The structure then functions as a façade of coordination.

6. Behind the façade, there remain two possibilities: there is little or no coordination or, more likely, coordination is provided by other means. After all, bureaucracy is only one way of concerting actions, especially in an institutional segment such as higher education, which historically has based itself in guilds and in many societies has much collegial authority rooted in expertise. We need to roam behind the bureaucratic scenery to see if there are other techniques at work.

Three
O L I G A R C H Y

Economy and efficiency are demonstrably not the prime purposes of public administration. . . . The basic issues of [governmental] organization and administration relate to power: who shall control it and to what ends?
> Harold Seidman, *Politics, Position & Power:*
> *The Dynamics of Federal Organization*

Proposition 10.6: When power is widely distributed, an *inner circle* emerges to conduct coalition business.
Proposition 10.7: The organization with dispersed bases of power is immobilized unless there exists an effective inner circle.
> James D. Thompson, *Organizations in Action*

Logrolling is the tactic most appropriate to the ends of small and relatively homogeneous units within a larger system. It is both simple and effective for the leaders of such units to exchange support for each others' demands.
> Grant McConnell, *Private Power and American Democracy*

One highly plausible conception of modern public services holds that balkanized administration goes hand in hand with control by constituency. The fragmenting of structure in the executive branch makes for narrower constituencies that are more able to influence heavily, even to control, the piece of government that is categorically tied to them.[1] As put by Grant McConnell: "The process amounts in some situations to the capture of government. However, it is not 'rule' as this is normally conceived; it is the fragmentation of rule and the conquest of pieces of governmental authority by different groups."[2] This thesis applies strongly to Italian public administration: the best analyses have highlighted (1) extensive balkanization and (2) great influence of specific clienteles upon particular agencies.[3] But, as noted in Chapter 2, the degree of influence will vary according to the status, power, and access of the clientele. When an interest group has high social status, much independent power, and clear lines of access to the bureaucracy, the balance between impartial legal rationality and biased interest-group service by officials will tilt toward the latter. Privileged access is the critical element in this tilt, and it can amount to the establishment of "permanent bridgeheads inside the system,"[4] with the likelihood that the protection of group interest will become a part of bureaucratic precedent and tradition. The bureau and the pressure group develop an organic relationship.

Constituencies and clienteles are generally assumed to be external groups interested in influencing those inside the government. But inside personnel also pursue group interests—"the bureaucratic struggle." Many modern, complex public agencies contain large groups whose members think of themselves as nonbureaucrats who must struggle against the officials, as in the case of doctors in state hospitals and teachers in public school systems in the United States. The members of such groups are in an unusual position: compared to external interest groups, they are guaranteed privileged access in the form of permanent positions within the system; at the same time, as self-construed nonbureaucrats, they can think of themselves as outside the organization qua bureaucracy, understanding that the central administrators are supposed to serve their needs so that the work can be done. The higher the consciousness of distinctive group competence and performance, as in the professions, the more the group members can seize the advantages of being simultaneously inside and outside—inside the boundaries of the organization and occupying crucial work positions but outside the realm of bureaucratic officialdom.

In any national system of education university professors are potentially a strong interest group of this kind. They hold basic internal position in chairs or departments—the fundamental units of organization. In the individual and collective exercise of power, they are ordinarily more important than students or parents and thus become, for the central bureaucracy, the most important constituency to please. At the same time, they possess imposing ideologies and self-conceptions concerning their place in society as scholars, teachers, and researchers which clearly set them apart from administrators and clerks. Then, too, the double balkanization of administrative domains achieved by professors in many national systems helps to wall them off in many important matters from the control of higher officials.

The position of senior professors in the Italian national system may be seen as a classic case of the capture of authority by an inside professional constituency. We cannot trace in great detail how this happened, since too much is still missing in historical scholarship, but we can show the structure through which the control is effected and identify several principal processes by which the structure came about. In so doing, we will see that the coordination of the system has been largely provided by oligarchical relations.

THE WORKINGS OF LOCAL PYRAMIDS

At the core of university autonomy in Italy, as elsewhere on the Continent, is the reality of professorial control over a domain. The chair is the source of this control. Simultaneously a position and a man, the chair is the basic unit of organization and an expression of individual character. The power of the chair may begin in formal rights, but it is circumscribed only by the limits of personal capacity to maneuver in intricate local and national webs of professional, administrative, and political relations.

Domain of the Chair

The power of the chair in Italy (and in Continental systems generally) is roughly equivalent to the domain of a department in the U.S. system (although everything within the domain of the chair centers on one position and one man). Just as the department is in charge of a specialized sector of teaching within the more encompassing administrative units, so is the chair in charge. And just as the department is the local expression of a discipline for purposes of research and scholarship, so is the chairholding professor. Since he *is* the senior staff, he is the only one with tenure at that level; all the others around him in the specialty are either nontenured or tenured as his assistants. His salary is considerably higher than all others in the domain, and his high status often brings considerably higher returns in external consulting and professional work. He is the repository for research funds given by public or private sources; in fact, traditionally the chairholder was the only one who could be responsible for such funds, since the junior staff were barred by national regulation. Until very recently too, the chairholder was the only one with voting rights in the more inclusive units of the faculty and the university. Thus, formal position alone has placed the chairholder at the peak of a local pyramid.

These local pyramids have varied considerably according to university size and prominence and the nature of fields of study. They have tended to be larger in larger universities and in those professional fields and scientific disciplines that require laboratories and teams of assistants; they have been small in scholarly fields more centered on individual scholarship—a situation that changed considerably in the 1960s, however, as dramatic expansion brought a great increase in numbers in many of the "softer" disciplines. Thus the realm of the chairholder ranges from a small domain in a peripheral faculty, where a professor has an assistant or two and a small number of students whom he may know well, to a large administrative structure in a major faculty in a central city, with platoons of assistants and hordes of students. In all cases, however, the chair has been the fundamental unit of organization, firmly entrenched in the national system.

Roles of the Chairholder

Crucial for understanding the Italian system is the way that the reach of the chair has been extended in all but the small, peripheral universities. The chair has been the centerpiece of a set of roles that are all occupied by the chairholder.

Institute director. The most important additional way for an Italian professor to carry out his academic work and extend his power once he possesses a chair has been to organize or take over a research institute within his own faculty and thereby become its director. If he cannot command his own institute, the next best thing is to be in charge of a sector within an institute and to rule the institute together with several other chairholders. The institute possibility is nearly always seized: In the 1960s, Italy had something on the order of 2,000 university institutes for its then 2,000 to 2,800 full professors—in actual count, about 1,980 institutes in 1960 (when professors numbered about 2,000) and 2,144 in 1967 (professors then numbered about 2,800). In the latter year, there were about 880 institutes in the sciences, more than 600 in medicine, and more than 600 in the social sciences and humanities.[5] In a survey at the end of the decade, 40 percent of the institutes had just one chairholder, with the majority having no more than three.[6] Institutes directed by more than one professor have developed particularly in the fields in which large laboratories and other complex facilities give room for the exercise of professorial prerogatives in heading a major sub-division (for example, medicine, engineering, and science).

The institute is the chief means by which a professor can reach for additional funds and thereby enhance his power. The funds allocated for teaching, in the form of stipends for assistants paid on national scales, are relatively fixed, and changes in amounts have to be argued and bargained for within the faculty and up the administrative structure. They rarely seem adequate.[7] Claiming a research function, the institute can apply for funds to the Ministry of Public Instruction, the National Research Council (*Consiglio Nazionale delle Ricerche*, or CNR), other public agencies, and private sources. Thus, "university institutes may obtain an additional income (which, in practice, is sometimes predominant in their research activities) from the C.N.R. or private firms.... C.N.R. contracts are made with a university professor or with an institute."[8] With such monies the professor can employ "research assistants," essentially without bargaining or checking with anyone. He can also legitimately use such funds to develop a library in the institute that will help his assistants in their research and attract students who need handy materials for their theses. In the years before the great expansion in numbers of students that gave professors more students than they wanted, status as well as claim on resources was usually enhanced by increasing the number of student advisees.

Institute personnel, ostensibly assembled for research alone, can be involved in a number of responsibilities. The professor can assign them to teach courses and to assist him in courses, as well as to engage in research projects. He can use them to help test students in the examination periods, the time when the workload is most onerous. As the assistants become more experienced, they supervise theses. And there are always things to be done at an institute other than research, or teaching as it is normally understood, especially in medicine, where so much time and energy must be devoted to clinical duties. A survey of assistants in Italian universities in the late 1960s elicited reports that they were spending less than half their time (45 percent) on personal study and research, with the balance going to a range of administrative and professional activities within the institute (33 percent) and to teaching (22 percent).[9] If anything, these reports exaggerated the time spent on research.[10] Among the faculties, assistants in medicine reported that a high proportion of their time (41 percent) goes to "professional work of the institute" alone, that is, to the clinical rounds, whereas assistants in the humanities and in teacher preparation put only 5 percent of their time into "professional work of the institute." In time devoted to teaching, the situation was reversed; assistants in letters and teaching institutes allocated over a third of their time (36 percent) to teaching, compared with 13 percent among medical assistants.[11] Thus, the institutes of different faculties mix duties in different ways, but in all cases the work of the chair and the institute become heavily intermingled.

It is not unusual in systems of higher education for funds earmarked for one purpose to be spent for a blend of duties. In the United States, regular funds for staff support in universities and colleges are defined publicly as going to teaching personnel, yet in many institutions departments have developed light teaching loads that permit time to be allocated to research and other purposes. In Italy, the high personal discretion of the chair-holding professor allows him, in his domain, also to blend duties of his staff by using various allocation screens, particularly that of the research function of the institute. Formal system and all, there is little or no accounting for how the professor spends the time of assistants who are charged to various accounts.

Since it is the main vehicle on the local scene by which the chair professor obtains more positions for his followers, the institute allows him systematically to enlarge his own pyramid. So wide-spread and so important is the device of the institute that it, rather than the chair, might be viewed as the basic unit of operation in the Italian system.[12] It is the place where most professors center their activities and deploy their assistants. However, the chair came first historically; it is the chairholding professor who establishes and controls an institute; and it is possession of the chair that gives the primary rights to control assistants and to participate with other influential persons in controlling the faculty and the university. Thus, we can view the role of institute director as an extension of the chair, a com-mingling of research and teaching in the person of the professor.

Journal editor. If possible, the professor becomes editor of a journal. Institutes often establish their own means of publishing articles written largely by institute members. For example, one inquiry in the field of sociology turned up eleven nationally circulated journals, nearly all quarterlies, at a time (1970) when in all of Italy the discipline possessed only thirteen chairholders and fewer than a hundred faculty members formally qualified by the state (in the status of *liberi docenti*) to teach in the discipline.[13] The in-house journal, representing largely the thought and work of the professor and those personally connected to him, is naturally not a "refereed" journal; papers are not sent out to scholars scattered at various places for judging on scholarly merit. The professor is the referee, with an interest in advancing the careers of his academic dependents as well as the name of his institute and his own welfare.

Dual appointments. Professors have traditionally also been free to teach in more than one faculty within their primary university or even to spread themselves among several universities. A sociology professor might hold a dual appointment in humanities and political science at his home base, or in political science at one place and in the teacher-education faculty at another, the second possibly located hundreds of kilometers from the first. Clearly, such multifaculty appointments widen the participation of the professor, giving him voice in a second (and sometimes a third) arena that includes control over positions for assistants. He enhances his capacity to move more people around and to do more for them while they are doing more for him.

Outside responsibilities. Finally, there has been additional elaboration of a set of roles through occupancy of outside positions. Traditionally, Italian professors do not spend full time at the university but instead participate heavily in outside work and come to the university for part of each week, or part of each month, or sometimes just for a small part of the year. In professional fields such as architecture, law, and medicine, they are in professional practice; scientists and engineers are found in business firms; and even social scientists and humanities professors have external responsibilities in publishing firms, journalism and other forms of communications, public bodies at all levels of government, and private commissions and boards. Italian professors have even been active in the national legislature while simultaneously holding university positions. When a professor is so active on the outside, often traveling extensively within the country, the senior assistants in the institute must carry the teaching and research programs. A professor's many involvements lead to his becoming the leader of an academic polity, carrying the burden of external relations for his group and offering general supervision of internal arrangements.

Personal patronage. But there is more: The chair-institute at important universities is geographically extended, reaching into the personnel structure of lesser institutions as the professor takes up the role of patron-sponsor. The key linkage is provided by the professor's placement of his assistants at other universities. Such moves are in their interests as well as his own. In the Italian system, dual (and occasionally triple) assignments are possible, and advantageous, for assistants as well as professors. A normal step in the career of a young Italian academic at one university is to go out to a minor university—one cannot step directly into a major place since the discipline is there in the hands of a different patron—but at the same time to remain a part of the home institute. In this way, a tenured assistant can maintain security at home base, while attempting to move up the career line by accepting the untenured rank of *professore incarico*, which formally entitles him to be in charge of courses out in the field. It is also common to be involved in secondary-school teaching, as

one of two or three responsibilities, using the income and possibly
the tenured security of the school post as a way of getting by until
a fruitful combination of university assignments can be worked
out. Thus the younger Italian academic, like his seniors, travels a
great deal. He must reach Cagliari on the island of Sardinia, or
Chieti or L'Aquila in the mountains of central Italy, or travel
between Rome in the center and Modena in the north, to teach or
test for several days at the field post and then get home to his
family and his assignments in the home institute. "National
system" in Italy, in actual practice, means personal accommodation, in weekly and monthly time schedules, to extensive
traveling.

For the assistant, the initial assignment is rarely a choice one.
He takes it as a necessary step and then begins his "anabasis," or
long march back. This is an effort in which persistence, patience,
and personal ties, and especially the power and goodwill of his
professor, may allow him to work his way back from the provinces
to a chair in a major university, *and* to a big city where consulting
is available, *and*, in the fullest success, to the place where he
already has his home or would like to establish one. Universities
that can offer all three rewards for many aspiring academics
include Naples in the south, Rome and Florence in the center,
and Bologna, Turin, and Milan in the north. There are also some
attractive smaller but historically noted places that permit easy
commuting from a home in the city: for example, one can live and
consult in Milan and commute to a position in Pavia, only some
40 kilometers to the south.

There are various roads from the periphery to the center. A
teacher at a peripheral place as an *incaricato* may try to have
himself called to a chair in a central university by placing well in a
national competition. He might instead ask that his faculty seek a
new chair for him and an appropriate competition through which
he, placing among the winners, might come to fill it. Once he
becomes part of the national pool of chairholders, he might be
able to transfer to a major university without the intrusion of
further formal competition. But none of the roads can be traveled
by using only formal means; the goodwill of senior people is
needed, particularly that of the chair professor whose institute
provides membership in a particular academic family.

Because of the geographical reach of the major chair-institute domains, there are predictable regional flows in the careers of academics and the assignment of personnel. In the late 1950s a survey of chairholding professors in each of the major faculties detailed the geography of their career mobility. Overall, the territorial mobility showed, in part, a northern circuit based primarily in Milan and Turin, a southern one around Naples, and a more diffuse one based in Rome.[14]

Another result of this geographical reach has been low staff commitment in the peripheral places. Small universities become satellites of major centers, used and often controlled by central chairholders. The academic who goes out but is unable to make the march back may well remain a field agent of the home cluster. There are always things that the patron professor can do for him—some research funds, some consulting, some additional teaching—or against him, by giving him little support or, in the extreme, disowning him and leaving him an orphan in the system. And the satellite locations do differ in how peripheral they are; therefore, a man unfortunately far out on the edge who cannot negotiate a full return to the major metropolis of his choice might at least hope to be brought in to a small city. It is when a man falls outside the extended cluster that he is alone and without hope. Becoming an "academic orphan" is a threatening prospect. The death of a mentor can mean that the assistant has much less possibility of getting ahead and may be forced to pursue a career outside of academia.

Other countries that use the chair as a primary unit of academic organization in inclusive regional and national systems have similarly developed a geographically extended cluster of personnel, as well as a local grouping, around the chair and the related institute. But the nature of the cluster is affected by the structure of the larger system and the way it distributes power. The Italian, German, and French systems have in common strict control by the professor over a local domain, with the professor historically the boss in his own shop. But the authority of the German chair is less extended geographically than that of the Italian or the French. In a decentralized system such as Germany's, based on provincial (*Land*) government, the young assistant moving out geographically and up the career steps need not rely so heavily on his former boss. He is independently recruited by a university and a *Land* government; he can bargain with them; and he will have resources in his new place, where he is independent of his old professor, with which to conduct research, teach, and build a cluster of his own.[15] In contrast, the French system is not subdivided by federalism but rather allows for patronage and personnel linkages, as in Italy, that have regional and even national scope within a unified personnel system—although, according to Terry Clark, the geographically extended clusters in France amount primarily to an informal linking of chairholders at different universities into a mutually supportive school of thought.[16]

The differences among the three countries appear to be more in degree than in kind, especially between Italy and France. The Italian system has some of the French pattern of informal linkage of chairholders. Younger academics who go out to another university, there occupy a chair, and then never come home again may well remain linked in a "school of thought" or, better, a network of power relations, with the original sponsoring professor. Some chairs, those that control more resources or that are more richly elaborated in a broad set of roles by their incumbents, will be dominant over others, just as in France a cluster of chairholders is likely to have one professor, usually in Paris, who is more equal than the others. However, of the three, the Italian system appears to have allowed for and encouraged elaboration of the chair in ways that build an autonomous cluster centered on one person, with a high degree of personal authority. Academic particularism in Italy is first of all rooted structurally in the organization of the chair-institute, which allows for the extension of personal power by a few.

Advantages of role multiplicity. We have been observing, then, a world of opposites. The position of the chair is a normal part of a *national* administrative structure, even more firmly fixed bureaucratically than is the American department within the smaller scope of the individual American university. The incumbent is appointed to the civil service, like other government officials and employees, and has rights and duties spelled out in national codes with the force of law behind them. Yet the professor is the opposite of the ideal typical civil servant, who comes under hierarchical supervision and follows the codified dictates of office. Upon appointment to a chair, the professor settles in as a person permanently in control of an administrative sector. The

control may be maintained over two, three, or four decades:
Traditionally, the Italian professor could remain in his chair until
death; when a retirement age was introduced in recent years, it
was set at seventy-five. This feature alone would encourage the
chairholder to become an academic *padrone*; numerous employees under him, holding statuses radically inferior to his, will
over the years become heavily dependent upon the man rather
than the office. And, from this base, the chairholder can
accumulate for himself a set of interlocking roles, inside and
outside the system, locally and on the national scene. Some of the
roles are formally defined, some may be quasi-formally recognized, and others are informally and sometimes unconsciously
assumed as part of traditional privilege. The powers of the chair,
then, give the incumbent the *discretion* to invent his own version
of a local monopoly. The accumulation of related and interlocking roles provides the *means* for establishing the monopoly
and giving it greater scope and depth. One notable outcome of
the role accumulation is the provision of some vertical and lateral
coordination within sizable pieces of the Italian system, in the form
of personal rule—essentially exchanges between superiors and
subordinates based on personal favor and loyalty.

Here are rich materials that bear on the sociological interpretation of social roles. The theoretical understanding of roles in the
past has emphasized role stress, the difficulty of performing
multiple roles.[17] The thesis was that the social structure drove
individuals into unwanted strain and conflict by forcing them to
take up numerous statuses and roles; individuals in these punish-
ing situations either sought escape from them or at least attempted to reduce the burdens caused by them. But clearly,
individuals in many settings struggle long and hard to multiply
their statuses and roles despite the trouble—in the form of
conflicting demands and overload of duties and responsibilities—
that they create for themselves in so doing. Adding and broad-
ening roles may bring personal gains that compensate for the
strain that is induced. The traditional Italian professor is a clear
case in point. His rewards have included: (1) an increase in
privileges in the form of more rights and liberties that come to be
recognized by others as intrinsic to the now-inflated complex of
roles; (2) an increase in status security, through the possessions of
more buffers against failure and greater opportunity to diversify

investments of time and energy; (3) an increase in resources with which to perform various roles, since he is better able to build a "capital" of role resources that can be used to meet various obligations and to make himself more invaluable to others, including dependents; and (4) an enrichment of personality, stemming from a sense of being needed, even fought over, by others and from a sheer presumption of superiority that attaches to one who possesses a wide repertoire of roles, has connections, and can do so many favors.[18] All this spells an increase in power, and it is not surprising that role accumulation is a frequently used tool in the exercise of power.

Such rewards for extending and multiplying one's statuses and roles vary greatly from one time and place to another. A hypothetical extreme case of the isolated, narrow role that does not need any of these rewards would be a hermit scientist studying rocks in a mountain retreat. Not so far from that extreme in real life is the completely specialized scientist whose total commitment to the laboratory precludes association with students or normal life in the family and community. Such a person may be rewarded by great accomplishment in the specialty while punished by a trained incapacity to enjoy normal human relationships and diversions. Somewhere near the other end of the continuum of role expansion in modern society is the married, urban-based Italian professor who runs a chair, an institute, and a journal; commutes between several faculties and universities; writes a column in a newspaper or a weekly magazine; appears on television; advises publishing firms; serves in the top management of one or more public and private agencies; and participates formally or informally in the formation of government policy in the legislature and the executive branch. His roles may indeed bring conflict and overload, but his cup runneth over with compensating rewards. His situational logic presses him toward the rewards of being a generalist whose involvements, in a seamless role, extend in every direction.

All this naturally makes for a hectic life, inclining the professor to borrow time from one commitment to use it for another. He is under systematic pressure not to linger in his teaching and to have others cover for him. He almost needs to stop the clock. In one interview, a young Italian academic joked that a professor's year means six months, his month is two weeks long, and his week is three days, his day is one hour, and his hour is forty-five minutes.

The Italian professor who narrowly restricts his role to the search for pure scholarship is likely to suffer many punishments. To the question (posed in interviews in this study), "Why can't a professor, securely tenured, crawl off in a corner, do his research, and write books?" knowledgeable Italians, whether junior or senior and inside or outside the system, told of how much damage he would do to himself, his discipline, his colleagues, and his students, in a system that pressed for role accumulation. He would throw away the power to assist others; students cannot afford the foolishness of allying themselves with a professor who cannot help them in academic and external careers. And, as he lost control of resources as well as the attachment of students, he would in time not even be able to help himself.

In net, the Italian chair has anchored a role system of great expandability. On balance such expansion has been functional for the chairholders, a structural ground for power monopoly. But its disadvantages for the system as a whole became considerable over time, as we discuss later.

Chair Control of Superiors

Beyond his personal pyramid, based on the chair and the institute, the Italian professor must relate locally to parallel units within his own faculty and then to the administration of the university. As described in Chapter 2, collegial authority that includes the election of officers shatters any possibility of strict hierarchical control. The chairholder and his peers exercise much influence on nominal superiors, the deans and the rector, by elevating them from within the group for short terms in office. Professors also sit with the elected heads in collegial bodies. Within each faculty, the ruling body is the Faculty Council (*Consiglio di Facoltà*), recognized as such in national law and regulation as well as in practice.[19] The council has the formal power to decide on all matters of teaching that fall within the discretion of the faculty, for example, the assignment of assistantships and the addition of complementary courses. Authority organized in this fashion ensures continuity and conservatism: among other effects, it almost rules out the possibility of major reform forced on the faculty by command from higher authority or by a reform-minded leader assigned from the outside to usher in some change. The council is much like the government of a guild, with the individual master as the basic unit of power and the aggregation of masters ensuring much "self-government" by using one of their own as chief administrator.

Similarly, at the university level of organization, professors have seen to it that they elect the *Rettore* from among themselves and surround him with collegial bodies in the form of the Academic Senate (*Senato Accademico*) and the Administrative Council (*Consiglio di Amministrazione*). The senate, the more powerful of the two bodies, has been essentially a guild federation. It is composed mainly of the elected heads of the faculties who, when they come together, are representing their faculties. The council contains some members appointed by local public and private bodies and two representatives of the national government as well as selected professors and the elected rector, but primacy of interest and influence has been assumed by the insiders—to the point of often making the council a mere satellite of the Academic Senate.[20]

Long terms in office through reelection are possible for both deans and rectors, but they are not guaranteed. Reelection depends on the incumbent's capacity to protect and extend resources, in the form of positions and funds, and otherwise to satisfy the internal constituencies. The dean has perhaps the stronger post of the two, since the *Facoltà* is a more natural cluster and a stronger functional unit than the *Università*. The dean is often already the most powerful chairholder in his faculty and, if successful in raising funds, enhances that power. The rector is less a fund raiser and more a general administrator for a loose federation of faculties. Rectors can be powerful, as when one who is already a chairholder of unusually high status, power, and personal drive is able to lobby so effectively in Rome to get special benefits for his own place that he is able to strengthen and thereby please a number of faculties at his university. For example, Carlo Bo, *Rettore* at the "free" University of Urbino for over a quarter of a century (since 1945), is widely considered a powerful and effective head. But it is more usual for the rector, while enjoying some honor and power from his office, to complain, rightly, that he is largely a paper-shuffler. He does not have the independent base of power of a president in an American university, or even that of a vice-chancellor in Britain, where an administrative sector is more clearly separated from the realm of the professors and given certain powers. For example, the rector does not have any formal authority of approval in connection with faculty requests to establish new chairs or fill vacant ones, but rather merely transmits the requests to the ministry. The rectors as a group do not have an organization of their own that would be a counterpart to the Rectors Conference in West Germany or the Council of University Presidents in France or the Committee of Vice Chancellors and Principals in Great Britain. And, of course, there are no trustees. The controlling unit is always a body of full professors who decide how to share marginal resources among themselves. This traditional understanding of who rightly should participate and dominate has become so entrenched that outside governmental and nongovernmental groups, given by national law a small number of places in the administrative councils, have often designated professors as their representatives.[21]

Since higher office is gained by election, the situation is inherently political. The primary contending interests are the highly autonomous clusters organized around the chair-institutes, each represented by its top man. The forces to be reckoned with in the larger polities are therefore the individual professors: their control of superiors through election is part of a general process of conflict and accommodation in a struggle among themselves. In place of bureaucratic coordination, the chairs are related to one another through one-man, one-vote membership on central councils that decide on the internal allocation of resources and any new actions. The self-interest of one pyramid is pitted against the self-interests of others, with each represented. Political exchanges must be made, for there is danger of open warfare if the existing balance of power, worked out over time, is altered. And in the closed-door meetings of councils and senates, the professors generally can afford to be pragmatic, making necessary exchanges and following tacit agreements, even if on the outside they have roles calling for an ideological stance and party loyalty. A Communist professor can negotiate directly with a Christian Democratic professor: a "Red Baron" can be a baron first and a Communist second.[22]

What finally forces chairholders to work together in a faculty is the necessity of uniting against outsiders and holding things together well enough so as not to attract attention that would invite intervention. Their common interest is the welfare of their small nation against other nations. If they cannot run their business in a way that does not upset the others, there is ultimate power at the center which may be moved to intervene. Normally, when maladjustments occur, it is unnecessary to have formal, open action by the top office of the system; preferably, all will negotiate behind the scenes, with an adjustment here and there that restores order. But when "necessary," intervention is open. In 1972, the Faculty of Architecture in the State University of Milan was, in effect, placed in national-system receivership. The faculty was a center of militant leftist thought, and a number of its professors and teachers, by giving examinations to groups of students and identical grades to all members of the groups, blatantly broke the minimal rules on how students are to be examined, that is, individually. The minister of education not only rolled back the change and declared the examinations void but also removed the offending members of the staff from their positions, including tenured personnel, and appointed an external committee to handle the receivership.

Thus, in Italy it is possible for local academic states to destroy or seriously to diminish themselves by so annoying other polities and the national center that they will be declared administratively bankrupt. But this is an infrequent, almost unheard of, happening. Normally the clusters know the boundaries of permissible behavior and stay within those lines. In voting alliances within the faculty and secondarily within the university, the professor-chaired pyramids make agreements that best allow the pursuit of mutual self-interest, through relations that are more collegial and political than bureaucratic in nature.

In sum, then, the Italian *Facoltà* and *Università* are not to be understood primarily as bureaucratic sectors, despite their formal position in a national agency and their subjection to national rules and regulations. Instead, they must be viewed as guilds and guild federations serving to protect and enhance the power of senior professors and operating largely through the mechanisms of conflict and accommodation that one expects in self-governing polities composed of varied, autonomous interests. The many roles of the chair include political action in ruling councils. The reach of the chairs includes control of the two important levels of organization above the chair itself—or essentially all local administration.

THE MEANS OF NATIONAL ACADEMIC OLIGARCHY

If within the Italian national system of higher education the bureaucratic lines of authority are weak and the local pyramids powerful, is there any national order, any national coordination? The would-be system has faced the problem of how to link together hundreds of local units, containing established faculties and the chair and institute clusters, that are secure in position and status. Linkages have indeed existed. However, these connections are not primarily a result of an administrative hierarchy within which a university coordinates its faculties and a higher body coordinates the universities. That would have required bureaucratic powers that have not been available. Rather, the answers to the problem of national linkage have taken the form of political tools, devices that have been constructed largely within the academic system itself. There is a national structure of coordination rooted in the capacity of the local academic chiefs to extend their influence upward to the national level, participating in decision-making at the center. That extension of influence has not been left to chance, even though it often appears so to outsiders. There are definite procedures within the system that promote strong national academic oligarchy; there are patterns of participation outside the system that enhance the oligarchy within; and there is a set of beliefs, ideologies, and doctrines that have served to make oligarchical rule natural and even proper.

National Academic Bodies

One of the finest ironies of the Italian system of higher education is the great extent to which oligarchy uses such democratic tools as popular election. Of course, this well-mastered strategy is natural to democracies based on highly limited suffrage. It is also common in modern one-party regimes and widespread in voluntary associations that, while formally electing officers, are suffused with conditions that promote Michels's "iron law of oligarchy."[23]

The Liberal conception of governance that went into the founding of the Italian state and that subsequently became traditional in Italian public administration saw power concentrated in the hands of the committed few who must legitimately lead the masses. The situation changed somewhat in the general political arena as suffrage was gradually extended. After World War II, voting rights were as inclusive as in other democracies. But the tendency to concentrate power in individual leaders and small blocs at the top has remained high inside the organizations that constitute the structure of the private and public sectors, from big business to the political parties.[24] The tendency has also remained very strong in the university world, with higher education as a subgovernment functioning as if directed by nineteenth-century Liberal principles of control. Just as it can be said that American higher education in the 1950s and 1960s was the last stronghold of free enterprise in the United States, with excessive competition and mobility of the labor force, so it can be said that the Italian university sector in those decades was a powerful stronghold of nineteenth-century Liberal government, with oligarchical leadership rooted in highly limited participation.

A key device in the systematic construction of national academic oligarchy has been the use of electoral machinery whereby local oligarchs select from among themselves those who will fill decision-making posts, in contrast to the bureaucratic process in which superiors appoint subordinates. That such a procedure should be operative at the local level is not surprising, since various forms of collegial authority that include the element of election are operating at local levels in one national system after another—for example, faculty members electing the master in an Oxford college and department members electing the chairman in some American universities. What exists in strong degree in Italy at the local level, as we have just seen, is a combination of a highly restricted electorate—the chairholders alone—and highly restricted discretion for the elected officials, the deans and rectors. But an even more outstanding characteristic of the Italian system is the existence of this general mode of operation at the national level, so that in virtually all matters of policy and personnel, judgments are made by a central council or committee composed largely of professors placed there by virtue of election by their peers. The authority of these professors becomes heavily intertwined with the authority of the permanent bureaucratic staff and political appointees at the center. After all, the formal basis for their authority is written into national law and administrative regulation; the bureaucratic staff holds the rule book and attempts to process papers accordingly. And the minister of education, a political appointee, can seek to serve the purposes of his party and his intraparty faction by maneuvering in and around the rules and norms of the system he is temporarily heading, most notably by simply delaying a decision or quietly managing not to initiate action on a competition for a chair or some other such crucial action. But the minister's role is "practically, a matter of little importance,"[25] since the solid ground of decision is occupied by the elected professors who man the councils and committees, the most important of which are the Superior Council and the National Research Council.

Superior Council. The most important single elected body is the Superior Council (*Consiglio Superiore*) of the Ministry of Public Instruction. Established originally as a group advisory to the minister, the council has come to have major powers and, with the minister, stands at the apex of the system. Attending to all of education, the council is divided into sections, including a section for higher education. Much of the work of this section has remained in the shadows of confidential discussion and non-public record, so that even knowledgeable Italian academics remain unsure about what it is doing and precisely how it goes about its business. However, enough is known to warrant the judgment that no major policies escape its deliberation and "recommendations." Its concurrence is considered necessary in all important policy matters, and those who have tried to follow its affairs reported in interviews that they were unable to recall cases—at least up to 1973—where the minister overruled the council and went his own way. No bureaucratic official within the ministry's Division of Higher Education had a position that was strong enough to enable him to attempt a change in policy without the approval of the council.

Most important, the Superior Council, through its higher education section, has been a primary source of influence in establishing and filling chairs, first by approving requests from faculties for national competitions to fill chairs and second by supervising the elections that select the members of the committees who will judge the competitions[26]—a crucial matter to which we shortly return. The council also has had veto power over changes in degree requirements and it has been thereby the primary power in maintaining the national curriculum described in Chapter 2. The nationally mandated courses protected and enhanced the power and status of certain fields over others, and certain professors over others. Since efforts to reform the curriculum have carried with them the threat of a major transference of power, it has mattered greatly what fields are represented on the Superior Council and which professors occupy those few prized seats. For example, a proposed reform in political science might seek to remove a course in constitutional law from the mandated list and to insert instead a course that emphasized a behavioral approach in modern political theory. If law professors serving on the Superior Council thought that not a good idea, their opposition would be sufficient to deny passage. The core national curriculum in Italy has been stable and conservative not because bureaucrats have resisted change but because a few national academics representing the main power blocs have been in a position to wield veto power. When they drew a line through a proposed new item in the curriculum, the deletion stuck, much to the frustration of those attempting curricular reform in various fields.

The higher education section of this extremely important general council, functioning somewhat as a combined personnel and curriculum committee for the entire set of universities, is composed largely of professors elected, for four-year terms, by all the chairholders in the system. A committee member may succeed himself for a second term if reelected; then, after a term off, he may serve additional terms. Candidates run openly, seeking support from academic factions and soliciting votes through personal and group appeals. The major academic fields have established rights to a certain number of seats in rough proportion to the number of chairs they hold in the national system. During the 1960s, the section consisted of eight professors appointed by the minister, twenty-four elected by the full professors, among whom four were from medicine, four from science, four from humanities, three from law, and one or two from each of the remaining fields, such as engineering, economics, and architecture, and three representatives elected from the lower teaching ranks.[27]

National Research Council. A similar system of election from the field has been followed in the National Research Council (CNR), which, through its allocation of research funds, has become the second most important source of support for the Italian universities. The CNR has operated mainly through a set of committees, numbering eleven in recent years, that have such disciplinary domains as physics or biology in the hard sciences and such broader groupings as economics, sociology, and statistics, or law and political science, in the social sciences.[28] The committees are composed largely of professors from the relevant fields who are elected for four-year terms.[29] Of 140 committee members, 72 are elected by professors in the same disciplines, 24 by junior staff, and 20 by researchers in nonacademic governmental research institutes; 12 are nominated by the government; and 12 are appointed by the other members.[30] As pointed out in an international report on science in Italy, "the present membership of these Committees corresponds very well with the existing university structure," a structure that exhibits "absolute predominance of Faculty Professors."[31] The appointed senior staff of the CNR itself contains active professors. Moreover, as the 1968 international report noted, the president of the CNR "is generally chosen from among University Professors; there seems to be a moral in this."[32] Finally, for the determination of the overall budget, the various committee heads, each elected by his committee, come together with the CNR president and several others in a *Consiglio Presidente*. Within its own budget allocation, each committee's judgment on the merits of research proposals is decisive. Thus the allocation of research funds moves toward control by the relatively narrow constituencies who receive the money.

Ad hoc committees. Although the higher education section of the Superior Council and the committees of the CNR are the crucial standing bodies that give professors great power at the national center, there are also important ad hoc committees for personnel selection. In reviewing the bureaucratic underpinnings of the national personnel system, we noted that no one becomes a chairholder in Italy without having entered and won a national competition (*concorso*) judged by a committee of full professors. And we noted that faculties can fill a vacant chair, new or old, not only by seeking to transfer a professor from somewhere else but also by asking the center for a new competition, which calls for the creation of a committee, or *commissione*. Such committees are not appointed but rather until recently were elected, one by one, through a process so complex that it defies full description. The Superior Council and the ministry first had to approve the request for a competition. Then, since a committee had to be established, and by election, the council had to decide on an appropriate electorate—that is, which disciplines within the university system were the allied fields from which men were to vote. The definition of suffrage may have been largely routine in certain long-established academic domains in medicine, law, and engineering, but it has often been problematic in the social sciences and the humanities, especially in new fields. If the opening is a chair in psychology, is biology an allied field? Political science? Law? There was room for discretion in many cases, and it was the professors on the council who decided on the appropriate electorate.[33] The choice of the voting base was an important step in itself, since different electorates favored at least different "schools of thought" in the particular discipline, if not different candidates.

With the electorate established, those professors who wished to be on the evaluation committee had to make their availability known to the voters. Politicking then became an open matter. Candidates wrote letters to friends, the telephone wires heated up, academic groups decided to back certain individuals and to pass the word around. If the field in question or an allied field contained a true superbaron, he could deliver a large bloc of votes for himself, his representative, or a favorite academic son among the other professors. Promises were exchanged as factions attempted to form a majority, particularly since other elections were occurring at the same time or soon after, and trade-offs among elections could be made. Election day eventually arrived, the defined electorate cast its ballots, and the five professors receiving the highest number of votes became the committee—so declared by the minister of public instruction.[34]

Once the committee meets, it must then open the competition, establish deadlines, receive applications and supporting papers from candidates, screen the impossible ones from the possibles, concentrate on examining the papers of the likely ones, and finally arrive at *la terna dei vincitori*—three candidates "graded in order of merit" as the winners in the competition—and so published by the ministry in its official bulletin.[35] Number one has the formal right to take the chair placed in competition, if he chooses, whereas the other two candidates have a formal claim during the following two years to fill chairs in the subject which may become vacant at other places. But formal rights are one thing, the reality of bargaining and politics is another. The university faculty where the vacant chair is located not only has the deepest interest in the matter but also commonly has a favorite and has been working for his candidacy. If their preference is ranked second or third, they need to get together with one or more faculties at other places to see if a mutually advantageous arrangement can be made: for example, for a second university to take the first winner, within the two-year grace period, allowing the first university to get the person it wants. Stalling for time is possible while such negotiations go on, and the first-ranked candidate will have reason to hold back if he is not wanted at the first institution. In this process several faculties coordinate their efforts to intrude upon the nationalized machinery for allocating key personnel. The nature of the contact is intensively political, as professors in one faculty approach those in another in search of a bargain.

The center of the political activity that swirls around a chair appointment is sometimes within the elected committee itself, which must deliberate in an atmosphere where the mood has been set by the politics of first forming the electorate and then electing the committee. Typically, committee members are voted in because they represent not only certain ways of thinking or schools of thought but also specific local clusters. At least a few of the five members on the committee are likely to be particularly interested in placing a man from their own cluster, or, at one remove, from the shop of a friend. Contrary to both bureaucratic impartiality and professional neutrality, the pressures for intensely political behavior at this point are very heavy. The five members on the committee must work to find the majority—it requires only three—who, in agreeing on the competence of applicants, will place favorites in one to three chairs of the system.

Sometimes the committee need argue hardly at all, since a majority vote for a particular candidate may have already been clearly arrived at when the committee members were elected. As in political parties and the general political arena, bargains can be and are made during the election campaign. Because such bargains are often made with a certain amount of secrecy, they are subject to rumors and jokes about precisely how and where they have been brought about. In several interviews, the young academics who were most likely to think that chair assignments are always decided ahead of time told the *Settebello* joke: that it is on the daily run of Italy's crack luxury train, the *Settebello*, from Milan to Rome through Bologna and Florence, that chair assignments (by competition and transfer) are informally decided —by the busy barons traveling among their many assignments and using the train as their political smoke-filled room.

The extent to which patrimonial politics has taken over from objective judgment—from selection without regard to person—is indicated by the capacity of academicians, legislators, and journalists to speak and write publicly about such matters without incurring libel for falsehood and character defamation. Naming persons and places, they have pointed to noted re-searchers and scholars who, they claim, have been denied chairs because they were outside the circle of sponsorship, or who have finally, after much squabbling, been given a chair in a minor university, as in the case of a Nobel Prize winner in medicine (Bovet)—which is roughly equivalent to telling an outstanding scientist in the United States that the only appointment open for him as a full professor is at a specified third-level university.[36] At the same time, the critics could spell out one case after another of "absolute favoritism" that landed the lesser-qualified in chairs. They sometimes predicted in writing all the winners in a field (chemistry, for example) a year or two in advance of the occasion, had the statement notarized, then had the notary open the envelope in the presence of journalists after the formal announce-ment.[37]

At other times, intense disagreement within the committee has been brought to public light by the committee's own unhappy minority. In one competition, two judges complained that more than half of the publications presented by one of the winners involved collaboration with one of the judges who formed the majority of three, and that the part written by each author was not specified. The minority went on to complain that the other two winners were clearly not deserving, to which the majority replied that it was everyday practice for a professor to become a member of the evaluating committee in order to safeguard the correct evaluation of his own student ("che il maestro entri come membro della commissione giudicatrice nei concorsi per tutelare l'esatta valutazione del proprio allievo").[38] And then, the critics claim, there are always the cases of the family relatives: the chair in cardiology that was finally opened up in Rome when the son of an academic notable in the same place became available to fill it; chairs in other fields, at Siena, Catania, Cagliari, and Genova, going to brothers, sons, sons-in-law, and nephews, with a total of nine out of eighteen chair winners in these four places being direct relatives of illustrious professors still in active service ("illustri professori attualmente in attività"), including a professor of law (Ermini) who was an ex-minister of public instruction.[39] In full fury and disdain, the critics referred to such personally influenced placement as the result of a Mafia of the chairholders ("la Mafia delle cattedre").

In such ways, alongside the minister of public instruction and on a more permanent basis than he, professors serve as national academics, controlling the commanding heights of the Italian university system. The lines of academic clustering run not only horizontally, from professors to protégés in the provinces, but also vertically, with professors in local roles connecting to professors (including themselves) in central roles. These horizontal and vertical lines are the strongest elements of coordination in the system. The vertical lines are especially noteworthy, since they are an extreme case of control of a sector of government by a professional interest group. Particularly in the personnel decisions of this particular governmental sector, we find control by professional peer groups that are within the formal administrative framework of the state and are able to use finely developed means of privileged access to power. These professionals also have virtually a "statutory right to determine how public funds are to be spent."[40] Not only are they consulted on the budget but they control the positions, at top and bottom, with the legitimate authority to spend the monies of the system.

Penetration of Government

Early in the field research that underlies this study, a knowledgeable staff member of a legislative committee (one who had been left an orphan in the academic world by the death of his patron) said: "You must understand, this is a professor-ridden society!"

In later interviews, one respondent after another pointed to how much professors involved themselves and exercised power in institutional sectors outside of education itself, in business, cultural affairs, and especially the government. Respondents would tick off the names of prime ministers and central political figures who had come out of the ranks of the chairholding professors, from De Gaspari, who was in power for eight years (1945–53) during the crucial period of postwar reconstruction, to Moro, Fanfani, and Leone in the late 1960s, some of whom continued to hold down their university chairs while involved full time in government. Other professors were in top positions in such important ministries as finance, as well as education, and in agencies involved in the development of the south. Professors have even appeared in top executive posts in Italian television, which is government-owned. Thus, more than in other major European countries and the United States, Italian professors have penetrated the executive branch of government. Their self-interest and point of view have created a permanent bridge-head inside the highest councils of the government.

University professors (and secondary school professors) have also participated in the Italian legislature. Serving there simply adds one more attractive position to the accumulating personal set of roles. Once in the legislature, appointment to committees is important, because the Italian Senate and Chamber of Deputies not only do their basic work in a highly differentiated set of committees, as in other modern legislatures, but also give the committees unusual strength in allowing them to pass legislation without submitting bills to the entire house. It is common procedure for the standing committees, acting *in sede deliberante*, to take final action: two-thirds of the bills introduced by the government and as high as 90 percent of the bills introduced by members of the parliament have followed this route in becoming law.[41] Even on large issues that must be reported back to the house, such as the approval of budgets, the deliberations and recommendations of the committee can be decisive. Without doubt, committee membership offers basic position and power for influencing policy, second only to the control of decision-making within the executive branch. And the parties, as well as individual members of party factions, can work together in committee more than in the larger legislative body,[42] since the committee is shielded from public scrutiny. It is a natural site for logrolling among truly embedded interests, a place where the pragmatic pursuit of self- and group-interest can have preference over ideological differences.

The education committees of the Italian legislature are manned largely by educators, administrators, and professors who are concurrently serving in the schools and the universities. The academics bring expertise; they are available, as members of a legislature in which the many political parties attempt to place their own subject-matter experts on appropriate committees;[43] and they represent the most powerful constituency. In 1968, the Senate's education committee was composed of thirty members, of whom twenty-one held a position in education (three were university professors and eighteen were teachers, deans, or inspectors from the lower levels). The education committee of the Chamber of Deputies at the time had forty-seven members, of whom nine were from the universities and twenty-eight were from the lower schools.[44] The committee members were drawn from the various political parties in rough proportion to their strength in the legislature: among the thirty members of the Senate committee, thirteen were Christian Democrats, seven were Communists, four were moderate Socialists, and the remaining six were scattered across five other parties. Such heavy penetration of the legislative chambers has put educational legislation primarily in the hands of educators; and, with the same logic of primacy of experts operating within the committee, legislation dealing with higher education has been shaped primarily by university professors.

This penetration of the legislature has helped ensure the conquest of a piece of governmental authority by the professors. Control of a segment of the legislature is thus linked to the balkanized bureau and professional constituency, which are themselves intimately connected. Such triple alliances are widespread in modern government, rooted in the interplay of growing expertise and proliferating group interest within the increasing scale of governmental activity. As far back as 1885, Woodrow Wilson noted how the workings of the committee system fragmented the American Congress: "Power is nowhere concentrated; it is rather deliberately and of set policy scattered amongst many small chiefs."[45] Recent observers have augmented this observation considerably, noting increasing systematic linkage between the several hundred "fiefdoms" of legislative subcommittees, specific executive bureaus, and related organized interest groups.[46] The Italian legislature leans heavily toward having its committees participate in such alliances—with, again, the case of higher education being an extreme one. Academic oligarchs not only have had primary influence within the relevant bureau but also have themselves sat on the committees that handle the relevant legislation. Legitimate possession of seats of influence in the national legislature has been the final stroke that firmly fixed power in position.

Clearly, the influence of Italian professors in their own domain and in Italian life generally is not an elusive phenomenon, nor is it simply a derivative of traditional deference to esteemed scholars and thinkers. Their power is rooted in their occupancy of a set of commanding positions, built up over time from the initial and still primary position of the chair.

The Right to Power

Such a prominent national oligarchy could not long be in power without a sustaining conception that legitimated its overt acts in the eyes of others and provided a sense of rightness within the group for covert decision-making. For such ideological support, the Italian academic oligarchy has been blessed with an embarrassment of riches, having at hand a number of traditions that have converged to give great confidence to the professor. Their rule has been supported by at least four sets of beliefs.

The Liberal tradition in Italy of elite leadership. This tradition has affected all institutional sectors of Italian life and has been strongly expressed in public and cultural affairs. "Democratic in its respect for human liberty," liberalism is generally "authoritarian in the importance it attaches to the necessity for skillful and practiced government."[47] It has fitted well the great discretion allowed men once they occupy a university chair and the extensive participation many of them achieve in prestigious roles in the general society. There has been every reason for Italian professors to feel like true members of an elite corps of leaders. They even clung in disproportionate numbers to the Liberal political party (*Partito liberale italiano*) which in the years immediately after World War II became "a weakly organized party of eminent personalities (its leader was Benedetto Croce), close to the monarchy and to the traditions of the pre-Fascist regime which they had dominated."[48]

The administrative tradition of state monopoly of "the public interest." This tradition, widespread on the Continent and encouraged in Italy by the Liberal approach to the building of the nation, became embedded over decades of expansion of governmental activity in the specific organizational arms of the executive branch. It helped to rule out any independent place for private groups which claimed they wanted to attend to the public interest: for example, private foundations were widely viewed with suspicion and constrained by taxing and regulatory powers of the government. As specific public interests became differentiated, they became the properties of specific bureaus within which experts on the government payroll would attend to them. For the higher education sector, there was little doubt that the senior professors were the appropriate experts.

The Crocean tradition in Italian philosophy and culture. Benedetto Croce (1866–1952) was a towering figure in Italian intellectual circles from 1900 until after World War II. His "historical idealism" served as the philosophic credo of educated Italians throughout that period: "For half a century he exercised a kind of benevolent dictatorship over Italian literary and philosophical life. Not since Goethe had any single individual dominated so completely the culture of a major European country."[49] Or, as put by another historian of Italy: "Croce never held an academic post, yet his academic influence was enormous. His fine style and universal grasp made him read or read about by all intelligent people, and he became a sort of secular anti-Pope, an uncrowned philosopher king."[50] He participated in public policy, joining the Italian Senate in 1910 on lifelong appointment, serving briefly as minister of education in 1920–21, and standing for decades as the leading intellectual figure in the Liberal party. So special was his status that the Fascists treated him as untouchable, leaving him free to criticize. As the Italians attempted to reconstruct a democratic state after 1944, he could, if inclined to politics, in all likelihood have headed the government. His believers and philosophical allies were everywhere in cultural positions and government posts.[51] His personal example was indeed that of the philosopher-king; his teachings, especially as diluted for practical use, were strong on intuition and "the pervasive role of a quasi-deity called 'the spirit.' "[52] Well-educated men, especially those destined to lead, should combine philosophy and history and individual creativity, shunning narrow training and especially the routine data-gathering of the natural and social sciences. The best men were broad in their sweep and enlivened by flashing personal judgment—an appropriate doctrine for the generalist professor in his many roles. Croceanism gave professors reason to feel that, placed among the elect to do much, when they used the authority inherent in their positions they were indeed serving society.

The conception of the university as a place where professors know best. The medieval ideal of the self-determining groups of scholars has been carried through to the twentieth century in the Italian university. The ideal was also updated and given a modern definition for all of Europe in the development of the German universities in the nineteenth century. Based in the Humboldtian conception of the university as an autonomous body of free research scholars, under state support, the German model has been given much credit around the world, in the twentieth as well as the nineteenth century, for the long preeminence of German research and higher learning. In addition, the German model added much modern vigor to the oldest ideals of the profession, emphasizing that the life of the scholar is centered on research and hence in his institute. The professor is such a central figure that the university exists first for him and only secondarily for the student as an apprentice in research. In placing such great value on the autonomous control of the chair, this widely admired and emulated approach provided substantial external validation for the power of the Italian professor. When Italian academics went abroad for study and academic contact, it was primarily to nearby, advanced Germany that they went, particularly from the major faculties of medicine, law, and the humanities, and especially in the period between World Wars I and II.[53] It was only natural, in the terms of this dominant Continental model, for professors to extend their control as much as they could, as universities became caught up in larger systems. They would be remiss in their duty to the community of scholars if they did not.

These doctrines, all favoring academic oligarchy, have given legitimacy to decidedly "nondemocratic" behavior; they have helped to tilt the vested interest of the chairholding role toward autocracy and collegial monopoly during the recent decades when democratic beliefs have grown stronger in the general thought of the country. The acid test of the interlocking strength of role and ideology is that in all the years since 1945 the chairholders of the Italian system have never raised their voices and used their power to roll back the extensive Fascist legislation that protected and enhanced their power.[54] And this was not because of a general political commitment to the Far Right: the chairholders, while conservative, have been increasingly and clearly in the broad middle of the political spectrum. Rather, within the higher education sector, the many converging elitist traditions became the rationale for oligarchical control by a professional group. It became natural to assume that, as a truly important person, the chairholder was to act as a cultural leader and tutor for the nation. The educational system at its highest level existed first of all to serve him; it should be shaped to his needs and by his dictates. The high status of the scholar of old was now bolstered and protected by modern formal structure.

THE TRIUMPH OF PARTICULARISM

Our review of how Italian chairholders exercise power has revealed a number of means by which personal rulership is heightened within a nominally bureaucratic setting:[55]

1. The formal system places each professor in charge of a domain of academic work and all the personnel within that domain. Such control at the operating level amounts to an extensive delegation of authority to a few thousand subchiefs.

2. The system enacts many laws and uniform codes but does not enforce them through checking-up procedures that would detect deviation, leaving an administrative open door for avoidance of rules. Bureaucratic standards are poorly supported in a structure of formal rewards and punishments.

3. The subchiefs themselves relate one operating unit to another, locally and nationally, by personally occupying a set of roles and by collegially selecting one another for administrative assignment. Personal rulership extends over related functions, such as teaching, research, and publication in a discipline; it extends over universities, as protégés in several places remain dependent on the patron; and it links local and national levels

(and external groups) as the one person moves among his various roles. Collegial rulership has even greater reach, as collectivities of professors choose temporary heads for local administration and also pick the members of national bodies holding primary power in critical decision-making.

4. Because of the great leverage of personal and collegial rulership, large chunks of the formal national administrative system can be used for defense of personal and small-group privilege instead of for its intended universalism. The professor is relatively free to become a *padrone*; the local collegial group, a set of *padroni*. The political processes and informal networks that have become natural modes of action allow for favoritism, cronyism, and bargained adjustment. The tools of particularism have even been built into and protected by the administrative structures and laws that were constructed to ensure the opposite.

If a national bureaucratic structure can protect and even administer particularism, it is only a short step to a sharper tenet: it may help cause it. Centralization always purports to strengthen universalism, but the outcome will be affected by the nature of the system to which the centralization is applied. Consider the following features of the Italian subgovernment of higher education: the key workers, the professors, are relatively autonomous; the administrative structure that brackets the country is relatively flat and loosely joined; "superiors" at several levels are elected for short terms in office; as elsewhere in academia, productivity standards are virtually absent, making it extremely difficult to identify competence and incompetence through administered standards; and centralization wipes out competition. Individual institutions do not autonomously compete for competence, nor do they find themselves with a competitive disadvantage if they suffer incompetence. Thus, centralization applied to higher education, as it exists in Italy, means that neither market mechanisms *nor* administered standards—as means available to penalize incompetence and reward competence—are strongly operative. In this context, the benefits of particularism, present in some degree in all academic and administered systems, grow stronger. For any participant, the advantages of being a crony outweigh those of being a neutral instrument of larger governmental policy. As the rewards of particularism ascend over the rewards of universalism, the self-interest of key participants often will be better served by being nonuniversalistic. The inducement is systemic and issues from the immediate administrative structure. To find causation, we need not speculate about the hidden hands of the church or the Mafia, or wonder about the modes of behavior that are supposedly buried deep in Mediterranean personality. Professors are so often academic barons in Italy because a unitary administrative framework has helped to make them so.

Crucial in the causal chain are (1) the weakness of administered standards, in the face of the indeterminacy of results in research and education, and the consequent power of the argument, rooted in tradition, that favors autonomous individual and group judgment, and (2) the weakness of competitive market mechanisms in the face of a state monopoly. In the Italian system, the state apparatus cannot concert the actions of the professors. At the same time, the state monopoly rules out the possibility of allocating resources and rewards through competition. What is left is considerably a patrimonial system within a state bureaucracy.[56]

If oligarchical particularism has triumphed over intended bureaucratic universalism, and if market forces have been largely laid to rest, there always remains the possibility that patronage and favoritism can be kept in place by professional forces, with behavior constrained by the internal standards of advanced fields of work. All expert groups have some impulse in this direction, at least a tendency to link self-interest and group-interest to common standards credible to the expert and the layman alike. This tendency had its origins many centuries ago in the self-policing capacity of guilds to hold members to certain rules; in the twentieth century it is embedded in the ideals and some of the practices of professional and scientific work. This aspect of modern expertise has been much remarked upon: the dominant social science conception of professions (including scientific work) has stressed the altruistic control of self-interest in the name of principled service to clients and society.[57] Clearly, professions attempt to construct barriers against "acquisitive and sometimes roguish instincts."[58] It can even be maintained that "the professions are the primary means by which reserves of disciplined generosity, once provided by the agencies of religion, can be mustered in a secular society, and one of the primary means (the nuclear family is another) by which persons of unequal statuses and powers can be united in bonds of trust."[59] But a profession can establish occupational integrity and other such socially desirable outcomes only if conditions favor the control of the "roguish instincts" of the individual practitioner. If the profession resides inside administrative agencies there must be favorable *organizational* conditions to effect this control.

Integrity will be diminished when a profession-in-an-organization has (1) large opportunities for corruption in discretionary performance of official duties, (2) elaborate hierarchies and shielded sites that encourage complicity in illicit actions and reduce external witnessing of them, and (3) inside control of the highest posts.[60] These conditions, we have seen, are common in Italian academic life. The chair's strong control over a domain of work offers large opportunities for corruption: a professor, if he so desires, can often make an assistant do his bidding, however improper, since he can independently mete out significant rewards and punishments. The chair-institute has been a shielded site, with little overlapping activity and membership with other chair-institutes; the councils that run the faculties and those responsible for the entire university have also been heavily shielded, having a few senior men meeting in private session. The central bodies of elected national academics have also exhibited this characteristic, operating in confidential deliberation. In general, the extensive balkanization of the whole system reduces "external witnessing." Moreover, it is difficult for subordinates to complain about exploitation and complicity in wrongdoing as there is little reward for the risks involved. Finally, inside control of the highest posts has been extremely strong. There has been no onsite apparatus of lay observation, let alone control, as exists in the boards of lay trustees in the United States. The bureaucratic machinery has been relatively weak and passive. When the professors were able to establish their oligarchical devices at the top of the system, layering this control over their already-shielded control at the middle and lower levels, the situational logic was one within which the academic profession would be unusually lenient toward, even biased in favor of, acquisitive and roguish instincts.

Our findings from the Italian scene fit recent revisionist

thought in the sociology of professions which asserts that altruistic operation of self-interest in professions should be treated as problematic rather than assumed.[61] In real life altruism may not dominate over the strong tendency of professional groups to behave in just the opposite way, seeking personal gain at the expense of others—not only clients but also junior people in the field and those who are in subordinate related professions. One needs only to consider modern American medicine to appreciate Eliot Freidson's excellent point that institutionalized expertise can give hierarchical control of the few over the many and can provide much leeway for the dominant professionals to be both particularistic in practice and imperialistic in relation to allied fields.[62]

The Italian structure not only directly taxes professional integrity but also indirectly weakens other crucial aspects of professionalization. Notably, within a scholarly discipline, it discourages associations that cut across universities to provide a specialized but universal bond. The personalized relations of the inward-looking chair amount to a bulwark against participation and cooperation within an academic society. The situation presses the chair-institute to be an inclusive miniature society, disseminating its own knowledge by running its own journal and operating as a placement office in which all major actions are controlled by one man. In this framework, young assistants have not found it rewarding to go to national meetings and there easily to exchange ideas, seek jobs, and applaud, on the basis of merit, the speeches of scholars, young and old, from other universities. They are basically dependent upon the sponsorship of their fathers in the local academic families rather than upon favorable judgment won on merit in a larger collectivity. Senior professors, in turn, have carried the chair mentality into the operation and tone of national professional bodies, often applying tight standards of admission that limit basic membership to themselves. Academic associations often have no headquarters office, no coordinating staff separate from the realms of the chairs. An annual meeting may consist of several papers presented by professors, with the assistants possibly allowed to come to hear the papers. Even weak disciplines that need all the bootstrap self-raising they can muster have found themselves unable to maintain effective association across the system. In such precarious disciplines as sociology attempts have been made to effect a common market of ideas, but the pull of the local clusters has been typically too strong. Those groupings that do take place within academic disciplines in Italy tend to be outside the professional societies. They occur when several chair-institutes within a geographical region find some common ground for joint efforts: for example, the support and staffing of an advanced training seminar.

A similar weakness in academic associations has been observed in France. There, too, a unitary national structure that depresses mobility and competition has been laid down over local chair organization that turns small clusters in upon themselves.[63] The differences between the two systems seem to make the Italian the more extreme case. France has a Paris that at least geographically concentrates talent and resourses whereas Italy spreads the limited talent among a number of magnet cities and thus geographically removes the clusters from one another. France has not elaborated the kind of machinery of national personnel selection that in Italy gives the local barons imposing national power that redoubles their local strength. But grouping the two cases suggests that the combination of chair power and national monopoly weakens professional linkage.

Probably the most serious consequence of the weakness of professional association is serious restriction on communication and the flow of ideas within academic fields. This consequence is particularly noteworthy in the advanced sciences which depend considerably on informal as well as formal relations across the boundaries of universities to accelerate discovery and the dissemination of new findings—scientific "communities," sometimes known as "invisible colleges."[64] If the chair clusters isolate themselves and draw impermeable boundaries around informal exchange, then the formation of larger invisible colleges is retarded: scientific knowledge is localized. And if the basic structure levies against exchange of scientific information through the medium of national association, then formal channels such as refereed journals, as well as informal channels, are weakened.

That the kinds of associations needed for scientific advance have been impaired in Italy is revealed in such specific problems as the physical mobility of researchers within the larger international scientific disciplines.[65] Here the first need is not so much the coverage of travel costs to international meetings as the freedom for a young aspiring scientist to go wherever the best training in his discipline happens to be at the time, whether in England, the United States, Japan, France, Germany, or Canada. Such freedom is not forbidden in Italy, and young Italians are found abroad even for a period of several years when attempting a Ph.D. after the *laurea*. But once the young scholar has begun to participate in an institute and has embarked on the complex web of assignments that will further his career, to leave for two years or even a year is to risk losing footage and right of place in career advancement. In interviews, young academics reported a preference not to be away more than six months, unless relations with the senior professor were quite secure and the professor was backing the idea of training abroad. At the senior level, Italian academics find that the affairs of local and national oligarchy are compelling and exhausting, turning their attention inward and offering much reason to stay home. And as so often happens under civil service, obtaining travel funds and official clearance for a leave of absence can be difficult. To some degree, all university systems offer resistance to an international cosmopolitan role in scientific advance, since there are always demands and rewards for local duties: stay home and teach instead of joining the academic jet set. The Italian structure makes the barriers substantial, in the weight of particularism in the local cluster and in the national structure.

Increasingly in recent years Italian science has been judged to be in a poor position to keep up with the rate of scientific advance in other societies.[66] The causes are many, from the general weight of humanistic learning in Italian universities to a low level of finance by the Italian government. Prominent among the causes, however, and in all likelihood the most important one, is the set of connected ways in which the national *organizational* structure of the Italian system is biased against the processes by which modern science develops. Of all the imposing consequences of the particularism of academic oligarchy, the weakening of the structural underpinning of modern scientific inquiry may be the most fateful in modernizing societies.

To summarize our interpretation of the nature of academic

control and coordination in Italy: chapter 2 estimated that national bureaucracy, as structured in Italy, could not coordinate effectively, particularly in matters of personnel and curriculum. In this chapter we have shown that coordination has been provided chiefly by negotiation and exchange within the ranks of the lords who by tradition *and* by formal position have been authorized to rule individually over bits of the countryside. An old elite system, locally rooted, worked out some national co-ordination by elaborating mechanisms of oligarchical connection between local and national levels and constructing devices for oligarchical interplay at the national center. Principles of oligarchical *authority* determine the structure of control; principles of oligarchical *politics* determine the processes of allocating position, resources, and power. Bureaucratic principles do intrude, but at a second level of importance, and bureaucratic rules amount to petty harassment of those who obtain and exercise power on other grounds. It is indeed then the case that the doctrines and practices of bureaucracy serve to mask oligarchical control. In so doing, they help to maintain the legitimacy of a purportedly public system in which much has been given to the private use of a few. In the following chapter we explore how this oligarchy reacted to the numerous stresses of a rapidly enlarged university system in the past decade or so—and to the concomitant pressures for fundamental changes in the power equation that, until recently, was weighted almost completely in favor of the senior chairholding professor.

Four
REFORM

These are sweeping reforms to propose, but then education in Italy needs to be reconstructed from the very bottom. We must remember from what a state of neglect, laxity, and bad government the start has to be made.

Matthew Arnold, *Schools and Universities on the Continent*

I say, then, that inasmuch as it is difficult to know these evils at their first origin, owing to an illusion which all new things are apt to produce, the wiser course is to temporize with such evils when they are recognized, instead of violently attacking them; for by temporizing with them they will either die out of themselves, or at least their worse results will be long deferred.

Niccolò Machiavelli, *The Discourses*

The direction which a reaction assumes is determined by the direction of the forces against which it reacts: the reformer is as much indebted to his environment as the conservative.

Hastings Rashdall, *The Universities of Europe in the Middle Ages*

The 1960s and early 1970s were a turbulent time in higher education in most advanced and developing societies. Consciousness and concern were everywhere raised by a host of problems. Conditioned by its own history and setting, each country had its special mix of those problems and had to attempt its own combination of adjustments. How did Italy fare? We begin by looking at the accelerated pressures for change that became known in reform rhetoric as "the new demands."

THE NEW DEMANDS

We may first dispose of two pressures for change which are supposed to be among the main environmental forces acting on systems of higher education but which operated only weakly in Italy during the 1960s. The first of these is manpower needs—"the 'suction' drawing graduates into employment and therefore influencing curricula and certification."[1]

The degree of manpower suction depends on the nature and stage of development of a particular economy at a particular time, the part played by the university in preparing trained persons, and the connection of the university to specific sectors of employment. The Italians experienced an "economic miracle" between the early 1950s and the late 1960s; yet there is no evidence that the rapid economic growth of that period involved in any way trained minds prepared by higher education. The Italian university has been dominated by humanistic and professional studies and only weakly oriented to business and commerce. Outside of a connection to a few scientific and engineering faculties, particularly the polytechnic institutes in Turin and Milan, Italian industrial management in turn has essentially kept its distance and has not looked to the university—whose graduates are ill-prepared for industry—for leadership material and technical ability. Thus, the reasons for "the greatest period of economic prosperity in all Italian history"[2] are to be found in more strictly economic factors, such as industrial concentration, entrepreneurship, low labor costs, and expansion of markets, aided by such political factors as American aid under the Marshall Plan and governmental policies that stabilized the currency, sponsored industrial renovation, and pressed for foreign trade. Italian industry was not then deep into high scientific technology and did not press hard for increasing the resources of the scientific and technological disciplines and for making other changes in university programs that would alter the balance of power among university fields of study.

Here was no obedient servant of industry but rather one among the many university systems of the world where industry laid little claim to graduates. The systematic disconnection between the university and industry was characterized well by the Organization for Economic Co-operation and Development's (OECD) "Brooks Report" (1968) on the state of scientific research in Italy:

> For reasons connected mainly with the mental outlook of the parties concerned ... co-operation between industry and the universities is very undeveloped. In 1963 only 1.7 per cent of research expenditure in higher education was financed by business firms. Industry rarely needs to call upon the university institutes. If a firm is small, it has little interest in fundamental research and is, in any event, not minded to contact the university; if it is powerful it endeavours to set up its own research laboratories in association, where appropriate, with competent academics. University teachers are often consulted in their individual capacity, by big business firms; but this is not so much an example of co-operation between industry and the university at the level of scientific research proper, as a sociological union between two categories of the Italian ruling class, university professors and the management of big business. [3]

In effect, then, the Italian professor "consulting" with industry substitutes a personal connection for an institutional one. Instead of industry coming to the university, there to support programs that would train students, the professor extends his personal role into industry.

Since university graduates have traditionally gone into government posts, particularly the national educational system, if there was any manpower suction it was to be found in schoolteaching. The movement into mass elementary and secondary education that came about so rapidly in the 1950s and early 1960s invited an increase in the output of the teacher-training establishments, the *Magistero* faculties. The consumer demand to prepare for teaching was also at the time being displaced upward to the university level by a growing failure of those trained only in the secondary schools to find jobs in the elementary schools. But quantitatively teacher training has long been a primary task of the system, and therefore the increased demand did not necessarily require a major structural change. The experience of other countries with teacher-training colleges, such as Great Britain and the United States, together with organizational thinking about the efficacy of differentiation, might have inspired the Italians to segregate an entire set of institutions for this massive operation, especially as preparation for elementary-school teaching moved up into higher education. But since the quasi-autonomous Italian faculties have so much organizational space between them, they compose a federative setting in which swollen teacher-training faculties could serve essentially as that separate set of institutions. Given this structure, the response to the demand for teachers was simply to expand a type of faculty already in place: Enrollment in the *Magistero* faculties rose from about 25,000 students in 1960 to 125,000 in 1970.[4] In addition, great expansion took place in the humanities and other faculties where students could also prepare for teaching positions. For an increasing number of graduates in a wide range of fields, an opportunity to teach in the mornings from nine to one—a "full-time" job in the schools—was an attractive basic part of the still common pattern of holding two or three positions.

The second major pressure with which we can quickly deal is the influence of the government itself, since higher education systems are increasingly "under the patronage, i.e., the ultimate financial control, of the state."[5] In response to a changing balance of political demands and to its own assessment of need, government will presumably enunciate new educational policies that will reshape old institutions and give rise to new ones. But complex reality can have it differently, as in Italy. There the university system has operated as a balkanized sphere of government, and the planning capacity of government in this realm has been weak. Moreover, academics have exercised much control at the center as well as the periphery, having penetrated the legislature and the executive branch to the point where they have heavily influenced government policy, in a setting of coalition government in which powerful factions can bring down the government when they are displeased. As a result, *this* government has not been inclined to articulate external demands and force them on the system. As we will see, the history of legislation to reform the universities throughout the crucial decade of 1958 to 1968 was one of failure of enactment.[6] The influence of the state as major patron worked to maintain the status quo.

Growth in Student Enrollment

If the economy and the government were not impelling forces for change, other forces did press hard on the traditional structure in ways that threatened a general breakdown. First in time and impact was increased customer demand,[7] articulated through growth in student enrollment. In the 1950s, the first effort to reform the educational system was that of enabling and inducing the mass of students to complete the primary and middle schools. The effort then moved up the line: to have larger proportions of the young continue into the various schools of the secondary level and finally to permit more schools at this level to have their students take secondary-school-leaving examinations and qualify for diplomas that admit to the university. The reforms of the 1950s and early 1960s at the lower levels helped to produce a great increase in student demand for higher education and a great expansion in university enrollment in the late 1960s. Enrollment increased from approximately 280,000 in 1960 to over 400,000 in 1965, to nearly 700,000 in 1970, and to 850,000 in 1973.[8]

As noted in Chapter 1 (see table 3) the expansion was uneven across the universities, with already large places becoming much larger while small places remained relatively small: Rome began to rival Paris in aggregating tens of thousands of students—its enrollment doubled during the 1960s and moved past 100,000 in the early 1970s; Naples surpassed 60,000. The increase was also quite uneven among the types of faculties, with great growth during the decade not only in teacher training but also in medicine (from 25,000 in 1960 to 79,000 in 1970), in contrast to minor expansion in economics and commerce (57,000 to 80,000) and law (50,000 to 67,000).[9]

Key to the impact of consumer demand, and strange to American eyes, was the lack of control over student input. However, the phenomenon has been a general one among Continental systems. Highly selective secondary schools determine elite selection, and secondary school graduates acquire a virtually untouchable right to enter higher education, there to have freedom of choice in selecting university, faculty, and field of study. As the secondary level moved from limited to mass numbers, and the right of entry remained unchanged, much larger waves of students washed into the universities and faculties in what amounted to an European version of open-door admission. Neither academic oligarchs nor governmental officials have been in a position to control the numbers and steer the traffic. Aggregate consumer demand has determined expansion with that demand also determining the magnitude of the task for different universities, faculties, chairs, and institutes. In a situation replete with oligarchical and bureaucratic controls, this demand has been a wild card in an otherwise stacked deck.

Expansion in Junior Staff

Expansion in the teaching staff became another important force for change in the structure of control and traditional practices. Staff expansion to some degree preceded student expansion as the system attempted to rebuild itself after the Fascist period and World War II. The total staff increased from about 14,300 in 1950 to 25,600 in 1960 (table 7). In that decade, the senior professors increased by only about 250 (from 1,744 to 1,993) while the nontenured *professori incaricati* increased by approximately 1,750, and the *assistenti* (tenured and nontenured) increased by 9,250. The already high ratio of staff-below-the-professor to the senior professor himself, approximately 7 to 1 in 1950, climbed to

TABLE 7: FACULTY EXPANSION, 1950-70

Teaching Rank[a]	1950	1960	1965	1970
Senior level				
(*professori di ruolo*)	1,744	1,993	2,597	3,348
Middle level				
(*professori incaricati*)	2,542	4,289	4,735	5,924
Junior level				
(*assistenti*)	10,059	19,315	25,577	27,350
Total	14,345	25,597	32,909	36,622

SOURCES: For 1950, 1960, and 1965, Organisation for Economic Cooperation and Development, *Quantitative Trends in Teaching Staff in Higher Education*, pp. 121-27; for 1970, *Annuario Statistico dell'Istruzione*, vol. 24, p. 17.
a. Categories established by the OECD staff for use in many countries. In Italy, there has been a large gap in formal status and privileges between the senior level and all lower ranks.

near 12 to 1. For the period 1950 to 1965, the average annual growth was 2.7 percent for full professors, 4.2 percent for the *incaricati*, and 6.4 percent for the *assistenti*; and in all fields of study the growth rates were highest for junior level teachers.[10] Even with the senior group expanding more rapidly during the 1960s, with an addition of more than 1,300, they remained outnumbered 10 to 1 in 1970 by the rest of the staff, whose numbers were swollen by 10,000 during the decade. With staff expansion thus taking the form of massification of the junior levels, operating hierarchies were changed in their general dimensions, becoming pyramids even broader at the base and more tapered at the top than they were before. Such structural changes were bound to create great pressures for adjustments in the traditional arrangement of status and power.

Organizational Needs of Modern Research

A third general force for fundamental change within the system as well as without was the nature of modern fields of knowledge, particularly the sciences, in which the rate of change in theory and method is high and the pace is forced by those nations that are in the forefront of a discipline at the time. There has been a growing pressure for such modern research structures as major laboratories that are steadily financed, securely organized, and structured internally to reward competence, even when exhibited by those who are young and hold junior rank. The ideal "research community" commits itself to creativity and hence to the organizational conditions that promote it. A young specialist able to come up with new findings is a prized commodity. The role of the senior generalist is to assemble talent, to set broad directions of effort, and then to turn the younger specialists loose to follow their hunches. Modern research also necessitates quick communication of results across a number of research groups, nationally and internationally, through publication, informal oral exchanges, and participation in national and international meetings.

Such growing organizational needs of modern science have exerted steady pressure for accommodation by academic structures in one country after another. And the pressure decidedly deepened in the quarter-century between 1945 and 1970 as science became Big Science and was more widely viewed as connected to national strength. The pressure was somewhat delayed in Italy, however. There, science on the whole was less developed than in Germany, France, and Britain; the country had seemingly more urgent needs in reconstruction and modernization; and the nonscience faculties at the university, autonomously pursuing self-interest, had no need to concern themselves with a retarded scientific estate. But the pressures were not to be permanently ignored: international comparisons became more invidious and scientists more vocal in their unhappiness. The OECD's "Brooks Reports"[11] was highly critical, putting on the international record what was already common knowledge among Italian scientists:

> The [Italian] Universities simply do not have enough resources.... only one third of [what] they need to do their job properly.... In this state of penury, research obviously comes off worst (p. 7).

> The fact remains that the present imperfections result in ... a state of affairs which is adverse to the development of teaching and research (p. 10).

> If teaching is hampered by plurality of employment and non-residence [of university personnel], research is even more so (p. 165).

> It must be recognized that there is no organized career for researchers in the Italian universities (p. 166).

By the late 1960s, leading science administrators and science writers in Italy were spreading their tales of woe in popular books, intellectual weeklies, and the Sunday supplements of leading newspapers;[12] they complained of an underfinancing of science, a loss of scientists to other countries, a porkbarrel distribution of research funds, and a university personnel structure that smothered the creativity of the young. The pressure of modern research upon academic control was not always as easily perceived by outsiders as was a doubling in the number of students or something as dramatic as a student strike. But it was steadily articulated by a growing number of natural and social scientists. At root the matter was enormously serious, involving big money, big power, and, ultimately, big politics—a time was coming when the claim would be made that national welfare was intertwined with the welfare of science.

What happens to science within a country is always part of the larger phenomenon of what happens to a wide array of fields of knowledge when subject to a so-called knowledge explosion, a vast outpouring of ideas and information that overwhelms the reach of the generalist and causes true competence to be defined in narrower segments. Personalistic hierarchies, as a general phenomenon, are strongly challenged, since the single boss commonly will not know enough to set the research agenda. Whole countries lose control over the pace of change in knowledge, since increasingly the specialties span nations and the rate of development is determined internationally. Thus, more broadly put, the third great pressure on the Italian academic structure was growing knowledge specialization, the organization of knowledge putting pressure on the organization of people whose work involves the cultivation and distribution of knowledge.

If we ask why the Italian academic system could not go on indefinitely with its traditional form of academic organization remaining essentially unmolested, the three pressures of student expansion, staff expansion, and knowledge specialization were fundamental among the forces of change that were to say it could not. There were other factors at work—such as increased articulation of egalitarian values and growing governmental concern over rising costs—to produce a long list of demands for reform. But crucial "demands" do not float around somewhere in the general culture (primarily in the rhetoric of educational conferences), abstracted from reality. They make themselves felt within the system as part of a generic trend, such as an increase in size of student body or staff, or as an interest articulated by groups with some power, such as the natural scientists. Demands not expressed in institutional trends or by powerful interests need not be responded to: the history of higher education in the United States and Europe shows many instances of the educational sector not responding for long periods of time to the so-called demands of a changing society. It is when demands infiltrate the system, either as part of basic dimensions of size and complexity or as part of the self-interest of important groups, that they are directly brought into play against the established ways. Then their effects radiate in different directions and trigger additional pressures. In turn, the outcomes will always depend on the nature of the traditional system and the responses that it makes. One way to understand the response of the traditional structure is to look first at the weaknesses of that structure, the chinks that would widen dangerously under the blows of the new demands.

VULNERABILITY AND CRISIS
Weaknesses of the Traditional System

First among systemic weaknesses was the extent to which the Italian structure of higher education failed to achieve internal coordination. When the scale of operations was small and educational change was gradual, the special fusion of oligarchy and bureaucracy that we have described could make necessary adjustments. But as the system grew even modestly in size and complexity, and encountered a somewhat faster pace of change in the surrounding society, the interlocking hands of oligarchy and bureaucracy were bound to constrict increasingly coordination within the system.

Even without the major expansion of recent years, the deficiencies of the old structure would have become telling. The elaboration of oligarchical ties, as professors attempted to reassert autonomy after the Fascist period, increasingly tipped the scales against rational adjustment in the performance of the bureaucracy, since the professors' arbitrary power precluded planning and official intervention. In turn, the passive bureaucratic observation of detailed rules and paper-processing also deepened, increasingly getting in the way of responsible performance in the academic oligarchy. With both oligarchy and bureaucracy inclined to stability over adaptability, their fusion strengthened both the disposition and the actual conditions for resistance to change. As rapidly changing Italy became a turbulent environment for its higher education sector, the firmly fixed, particularized control that was characteristic of the old structure became the potential Achilles' heel of the system.

The traditional system was also increasingly vulnerable through its tight limitations on participation. Tension between hierarchical organization and extensive participation of lower members is particularly apparent in the control of academic systems since there the collegial ideal of self-governing scholarly communities encounters bureaucratic authority, trusteeship (in some systems), and governmental determination of the public interest—all of which dictate supervision from the top. The problem becomes much more severe when remote control by high levels in a national system is coupled with control by a few at the local level where "self-government" is supposed to work. The great bulk of the teaching force is then under the heel of tight hierarchies within large hierarchies. As the ranks of junior academics swelled, their lack of participation in the affairs of the faculties and universities would be felt more and more as intolerable. (Again, international comparisons became invidious: young Italian academics who had visited in American departments could report much greater self-direction and participation in collegial rule for junior staff than was granted by the Italian chairs and institutes.)

Moreover, as the Italian population became further schooled in democratic ideals and forms of democratic participation in other institutional arenas, particularly after the Fascist period, the highly limited suffrage in higher education would sooner or later become an obvious anachronism. It was only a matter of time before the extensive powers of the professors would seem like a medieval throwback, with the label of "i baroni" increasingly affixed as a nasty epithet. Sharply limited participation in governance became a major vulnerability not only because the system moved from elite education toward mass involvement but also because more segments of the general population were bound to recognize that schooling in oligarchy is hardly the way to prepare leaders and citizens for a democracy.

A third problem inherent in the traditional structure was the pronounced weakness of formal administration. The major inclusive units of membership for teachers and students alike, the faculties, have been poorly linked by administrative means to one another, within the same university as well as within the same fields at other universities. We noted also the weak linkage of professors; professional organization has not been able to compensate for the coordinating weaknesses of bureaucratic organization. Even if the resistance of oligarchs were left aside, planned change in the Italian system would flounder at the interface between university and faculty. At that point, the structure is inadequate for implementing change from the top down. A university that is a loose collection of faculties is not structurally a modern university, in the sense of orderly capacity to react to the modern rate of change, especially when expansion in size *increases* the looseness of connection among the faculties.

Further, informal negotiation and exchanges have grown as the means of filling the near vacuum of formal coordination. As informal adjustments have become institutionalized as a way to get things done, the circuit is completed: professors who are successful in making do informally are confirmed in their view that the best thing to do with formal coordination is to minimize it. Little self-interest is generated to develop a planning capacity, since an effective planning office in the ministry would certainly raise questions about the old structure in the process of recommending new institutions and programs, and hence would intrude upon the hidden powers of the established parties. Central planners everywhere tend to have only small supporting constituencies. In Italian higher education, a central planner has been lonely indeed, a David without a slingshot up against the Goliath of the 3,000 chair professors.

Finally, the traditional system has been characterized by an absence of competition which might impel adaptations through the flow of personnel and clients from one place to another. Not only does the structure permit little competition for individual talent and institutional status based on talent, but in addition the Italian fusion of academic oligarchy and state bureaucracy is virtually the ideal system for suppressing competition among operating units. Market dynamics are thereby weakened, a weakness joined to those of planning and administrative coordination. Thus, another important mechanism for system adaptation to new demands and external pressures is greatly reduced if not knocked out. In economic terms, higher education in Italy may be seen as a system strewn with barriers to competition: a monopoly controlled by an oligarchy through a bureaucracy.

Impact of the New Demands

The sum of these weaknesses is a unitary national framework for higher education that (1) is rigid because of the interlocking of academic oligarchy with state bureaucracy, (2) allows extremely limited participation in decision-making for the great bulk of the teaching staff, (3) possesses minimal capacity for formal coordination, and (4) permits little distribution of staff and resources through competition. With these vulnerabilities in mind, we turn back to the new demands of recent years and pursue the interaction of the new and the old that has led to crisis. By 1970, the Italian system clearly was being faced with demands for which it had little preparation and little capacity for adjustment. The impact of the new demands on the traditional structure had at least the following five results: an overloading of the operating units; an overloading of the linkages that held the operating units together in a national system; a deepening deprivation in research structure; a growing incapacity to cope with discontent; and a mounting justification for external intervention.

Overloading of the chair-institute. In Chapter 3, we described in considerable detail the accumulation of roles of the Italian professor that thereby enhanced his personal power. Professors have tended to stretch themselves thin, pulling time and energy from one responsibility to invest in another. Even in the best of circumstances, professors were likely to be very busy, racing around to keep up with minimal requirements of teaching, administration, examination, and research—all of these internal duties together receiving only part-time attention as external affairs were attended to. The effect of the great student and junior staff expansion was to multiply the burden of all the basic responsibilities and thereby overload the traditional role monopoly of the professor.

Consider the requirements of teaching. For a while, increasing numbers of students could be handled by moving to a larger lecture hall, especially since many students do not come to lectures anyway and will try to pass the examination by means of syllabi, tutoring, group study, and luck. But soon there were too many for a teacher even to pretend that they could be scheduled for a single time and place. Other lectures had to be added. Then, too, as growing knowledge specialization and widening student interest pressed for more specialized courses to be given as basic courses in nearly every discipline, these also had to be scheduled and manned. The professor clearly could not do it all, even if he wanted to, and he has relinquished the traditional role of always giving the basic courses in his field. Under these circumstances, those in the first two strata below the chair-holders, the *professori incaricati* and the senior *assistenti*, not only increased greatly in number but moved into important teaching responsibilities, such as teaching basic courses, and thereby undercut the distinction in teaching role between the chair and the others. In the eyes of students, those who carried the teaching duties of professors looked like professors. This reallocation of duties naturally made the radical split in status, privilege, and reward harder to maintain; the battle cry of the *professori incaricati* was that they were doing the work without the rewards.

Operational overload became most striking in the crucial business of examination. By the end of the 1960s, the professor in the large university, especially the University of Rome, was under heavy pressure to be testing or to be available for testing much of the time. To examine the ever larger crowds of students by means of the traditional oral individual session could mean weeks of time for each of the three annual examination periods. Testing time could affect teaching time as well as research time. By 1970, Italian academics could report one case after another at the major universities where the chair faced the problem of how to test, one by one, hundreds or even a thousand or more students annually. In those cases, any pretense to rationality was gone: the examination system was such a burden for everyone and so twisted in practice that something would have to give.

The institute came under similar pressures of overload. The assistant has to have a place there, since his career depends on early research productivity and on getting a professor's recognition and support. His self-interest demands the personal attention of the professor, and tradition says he should have it. But considerable expansion made this difficult and often impossible. The institute became more stratified, with assistants under assistants, as the senior ones assumed major responsibilities in teaching and research. The number of *dottori* simply became too large for all to have a direct personal relation with the patron professor.

Such overloading, then, has driven the Italian professor toward becoming a remote manager of a large domain of teaching, testing, and research, leaving him unable to maintain traditional personal relations. Faced with droves of students, he cannot individually supervise the thesis. He cannot personally identify the talented students who should be encouraged and supported to go beyond the *laurea*, as he traditionally prided himself on doing. In extreme cases, he can disappear from view altogether: stories abound among students in Rome of never having even seen the head man in the lectures—because either he was not there, or they were not, at the scheduled times. The situation shatters what remained of the traditional images of the leisurely professor-apprentice relation, to which only a few are called in the elite university, and of the great lecturer thrilling the rapt audience that eagerly soaks up his wisdom. The gap between ideal and reality that always existed is so widened that occasional congruence and wishful thinking will not span it. Too often do the assistants appear in the lecture hall to lecture in place of the professor; too often does the student obtain only hurried, infrequent consultation even with an assistant. In turn, the junior staff can no longer find the personal connection to the chairholder that the career line makes imperative. And the chairholder himself is imprisoned by the new reality. He has the formal authority to do largely as he pleases in his own realm, but the overload brought about by the failure of rigid structure to adapt to the new pressures restructures his work and so absorbs time that his discretion becomes limited. In such ways expansion into mass education overwhelms a traditional structure rooted in the particular and the personal. Overload presses the actors in the situation, in self-defense, to find new ways of structuring everyday relations, with or without the sanction of legislative act and national rule.

Overloading of the national links. The greatly increased scale of organization that followed from the student and staff expansion also caused a vast overloading of the linkages between the local units and the central national bodies, that is, the bureaucratic and oligarchical networks of vertical integration. On the bureaucratic side, a national system that purports to be administered by impartial rule has a propensity to gradually elaborate the rules. As expansion and specialization have led to greater complexity, there has been in Italy a great increase in rule specification and rule enforcement. Funds are disbursed to many more people (students and staffs) in many more categories (for example, among different levels of teaching staff) and through more channels, such as research-grant lines and scholarship offices. The funds feeding into a given institute may take many routes from government offices. In a national structure long weak in coordination at the university and faculty levels, accountability erratically runs the gamut from tight accounting for pennies to no accounting for thousands of dollars. Research students in Rome may need to retain a ticket stub for each eight-cent bus ride, while institute directors may not need to document expenditures for antique furniture and other exquisite office furnishings out of a sizable research grant. Confidence and respect decline accordingly. And, as elsewhere in mammoth bureaucracies—for example, the New York City school system—there is a loss of confidence in the formal scheme as overload causes traditional channels of clearance and reimbursement to become ever slower. The impulse to maneuver is thereby strengthened: the only rational course is to evade the rules. For example, to move ahead in its work a scientific institute may decide it must bootleg equipment, charging it off a little here and a little there on a set of accounts variously named. The expansion of inputs into the traditional bureaucratic structure of the university system during the 1960s made it one of the public sectors widely judged to be sick—"choking itself" administratively, as respondents put it.

We have emphasized how much an academic oligarchy has managed to coordinate the Italian system. Therefore, it is possible that, if the bureaucracy tended to break down, the national oligarchs might cleverly and adaptively fill the breach. They have long practiced how to zigzag through a maze of conflicting rules and ambiguous standards, staying on their feet in situations that would defeat the untutored and less clever. But, in a system that has depended so much on personal bargaining, alliance, and trade-off, the oligarchs themselves have become increasingly overwhelmed by growing scale. They cannot maintain their traditional personal integration of control as the number of transactions increases manyfold. Even the national selection system has become so overloaded that it falls behind in getting persons into the positions it takes so much trouble to create. The bottleneck of an elaborately arranged ad hoc committee for particular selections is essentially a "craft" approach in a situation calling for mass production. Then, too, knowledge specialization and the modern rate of change have directly challenged the centralized curriculum. What national committee of academics anywhere could possibly keep abreast of all the changes needed in all the disciplines, even with subcommittees piled upon subcommittees? Since the senior men in Italy were disposed to keep their own numbers highly limited, they were bound to lose the capacity to dispense enough particularism to keep the old system working well. The national linkage as well as local operations thus slid toward crisis.

Deprivation in research structure. Earlier we pointed to the extent to which the Italian academic structure has become basically antithetical to the needs of modern science. The balkanized clusters have remained under the arbitrary authority of senior generalists; young scholars have not been able to break away from patronage; oligarchs in a discipline control research expenditures nationally, constrain new directions of effort, and keep down parallel research structures outside the university that would drain funds from the university institutes. Young scholars, discouraged by it all, reluctantly leave for other countries, accepting posts in Edinburgh or Berkeley, and the international scientific community issues critical reports. Of all modern bodies of thought, scientific judgment is the most committed to universalistic canons that challenge the endemic particularism of Italian academic life. The thrust of those canons has been blunted, defeated, and ignored, especially by long entrenched sectors of the professoriate that prefer a humanistic university. But the canons always insistently return, within the faculties of natural science, medicine, engineering, and the social sciences. For the nation to move into full membership in the European family of advanced nations, to leave completely behind the status of a Mediterranean stepchild, it must attend to science and technology as well as industrialization, and it must develop these either inside or outside the university or both. The sense—at least among scientific personnel—of growing shortage of a support structure for modern science has helped move the Italian university system toward crisis.

Incapacity to cope with discontent. Without doubt, the most dramatic events in Italian higher education in the late 1960s and early 1970s were the serious student disruptions at nearly every major university, especially during the academic years 1967–68 and 1968–69. Militant student organizing spread from the new Sociology Institute in the city of Trento to the University of Turin and then on to Milan, Rome, and the other major centers. Universities were occupied and classes suspended for long periods of time: During 1968–69 the University of Rome saw only about three months of regular classes in many of its faculties.[13] Physical damage was extensive, and personal injury common enough as students vandalized some buildings and fought with the police, and occasionally among themselves, in numerous skirmishes in and around the universities. Professors were personally confronted, challenged face-to-face, in ways they could not even imagine before. The student movement proceeded rapidly through several stages of development, and by 1972, as in other countries, it ended up badly split, exhausted, and no longer in the headlines.[14] Its impact remains unclear: its direct influence on the basic structure of control seems slight; its indirect influence for long-run change may have been considerably greater, by changing the attitudes of some professors, especially the younger ones, and by encouraging the junior staff, better positioned than the students within the gates of the university, to be more discontented and to organize for persistent protest.

The causes of the student discontent also remain unclear, as in other countries. Explanations have pointed to the problems of youth in modern industrial society, to ideological and political concerns that are largely external to the university, and to internal structural features. The best analysis of student protest in Italy has shown that the students were first of all concerned with "the huge structural problems which affected Italian universities, and that the Italian Student Union (UNURI) in the 1950s and early 1960s had seen its main struggle to be for the 'improvement of the academic structures.' "[15] The rapid expansion of enrollment after 1965 brought with it not a great surge of student optimism over new opportunities but a serious worsening of the student situation which was bound to increase anxiety. Quarters were crowded; lagging staff expansion left the students more out of touch with staff members and especially the senior professors; and financial support of students was weak and uneven. In the days of elite enrollment, up to the 1960s, student displeasure was either silenced by the intimidation of authority, or accommodated in the personal channels of the balkanized domains within which the students fell, or expressed in the political activities of the many student associations, which, by virtue of their connection to the political parties, were considered training grounds for entry into politics. When students did break out into mass action, even to take on the police in the piazza, their battalions were relatively small. Expansion toward mass higher education changed all this: there were many more students who were more unhappy and alienated; the old particularistic channels were severely overloaded and far less usable; and the increase in numbers swelled the promise of mass action.

What is especially clear is that expansion transformed elite discontent into mass discontent in a university poorly equipped to handle active protest. The great administrative weakness of the university and the faculty left these units virtually incapable of coping with military group action, this side of the ultimate step of calling in the police. During the 1960s, in a number of countries, academic senates and collegial bodies generally proved that they were ponderous elephants, not capable of the fast steps needed in day-by-day bargaining and maneuvering against opponents who would not observe the old rules. The Italian academic councils were extremely inept, offering amateur administrators equipped with only limited discretion and inadequate staff. In the depths of their troubles in the late 1960s, the senior professors felt powerless and hopeless, not knowing what to do other than to use police power. Often, too, they were stung to the quick by the students' tactic of personal insult. But student power burned out first, for it was unrooted power, while the enormous momentum of deeply rooted power persisted. The lashing-out subsided into an occasional angry burst, and everyone returned to the normal business of trying to make do within an increasingly overloaded structure.

By 1970, Italian higher education had moved into a stage where no one seemed in control. No one was able to control the general expansion in numbers, not even the expansion of the individual university nor, in most cases, the individual faculty. The admission machinery was in bad repair: the secondary system sent through the many rather than the few, and the university system, caught in its own incapacity to effect major changes and pressed to offer wider admission by democratic ideology, now given muscle by the parties of the Center and the Left, was unable to assemble new gatekeepers and to steer the increased student traffic within the system. The secondary school was now a much broader highway, leading up to the time-worn, narrow streets of the old city that was the university. The Italian experience suggests that in the transition from elite to mass higher education, tight control of internal structure without control over inputs of the system will lead to structural overload that produces a breakdown in control. When traditional forms are unable to cope and new forms are blocked from emerging, paralysis ensues. The system is then in a stage of institutional insufficiency.

Growing justification for external intervention. Apparent paralysis in an important bureau calls for attention from the central councils of government. As we have stressed, the structure of government in Italy has made effective intervention difficult and unlikely. The academic oligarchs have exercised significant influence in the legislature and parts of the executive branch, besides controlling from internal sites the sector of which they are a part. And whatever the policy that might pass through the highest councils of government, implementation has been so completely in the hands of the senior professors that their opposition would ensure, if not policy failure, then at least serious attenuation. What could come out, if anything, would look different from what went in—an old but now ever more serious problem in governmental administration, which can be seen in an extreme form in the setting we have examined.[16] Thus, apart from itself being overloaded with a wide range of pressing social and economic problems, the Italian government had to fear opposition and failure if it tried to intrude into a sector so unable to cope with its own problems.

But the growing crisis of traditional structure seemed to demand intervention. If it is hard to do anything with such a structure, it is also impossible to leave it alone. The ultimate threat to the established academic oligarchy posed by the collision of the new demands and the traditional structure was a wider politicization of issues. The student movement and the conservative reaction to it encouraged more groups to intrude into the normal politics of the system. And the justification for external intervention was increasing on other fundamental grounds, such as the condition of science. Thus, even if student action cooled, as it did, the government would still have to raise the priority of higher education problems. The training ground of the governmental elite could not be readily written off, assigned to the terminal ward, even if some functions such as scientific research were to be moved gradually outside the structure. Even the self-interest of tradition-minded professors would finally dictate some accommodation, as the balance of forces in the larger political setting as well as within their administered domain slowly shifted against them. Some changes had to be made. But what changes?

The Character of Change

We can quickly identify three ideal directions of structural reform that would modify the Italian structure to accommodate various new demands and repair the weaknesses of the traditional arrangements.

Decentralization. A structure suffering from oligarchical and bureaucratic rigidity within a state monopoly needs first to be broken up. The primary means of doing so is decentralization of ownership and formal control to lower levels of government: power to the region, province, and city. Since the Italian government has been edging toward some regional decentralization, the university sector could be made a part of this general effort. Beyond partially breaking up the existing national bureaucracy and undermining the national academic oligarchy, regional control may also possibly bring some competition into the system. Also, the small private sector could be further encouraged.

Institutional differentiation. The university monopoly could be broken by the creation of new institutional sectors—for example, technological colleges, research institutes, and short-cycle units. If some pluralism of sectors and forms were introduced, the university could be relieved of certain demands, student and staff choice among alternatives could be widened, and perhaps some modern intersector competition could be brought into play. Those who plan would do so for differentiation, rather than uniformity, and for new structures devoted to innovation, modern research, and the promotion of attractive job opportunities within higher education as alternatives to employment in the old universities.

Internal reorganization. A structure suffering from administrative weakness at its middle levels and heavy but fragmented power at its lower levels needs strengthening of the middle, which would reduce narrowly localized power and also pull some authority from the national center down to the university. Strengthening of the middle could possibly be effected by new or revamped collegial councils of the university and the faculty, designed particularly to increase the participation of junior faculty and students in broad policy deliberation, thereby restoring eroded legitimacy of governance at these levels. But the principal route lies in the building of administrative capacity in the form of more permanent academic officers who would have power to mediate between the national academic bodies and the local faculty clusters and to reduce the fragmentation of power at the local level. Excessive chair power could also be reduced by such moves as replacing chairs with departments as the primary units of organization and introducing a graduated rank structure that would put more tenured middle faculty between the junior faculty and the senior professors.

In addition to these major directions of reform, aimed to reduce current rigidity, increase participation, strengthen coordination, and initiate competition, another step might be to take professors out of the national civil service, since the legal-administrative status of the academic staff is in itself an important obstacle to the goals of reform. Overall the objective would be a more varied and flexible system that could respond not only to the demands of the current period but also to future demands yet unforeseen. But such ideal and imagined possibilities are likely to be largely the stuff of dreamers. Let us turn instead to the actual events of reform and then judge how change comes about and whether clear-cut directions of effort are possible.

Pressures for Legislation

As far back as 1958, ministers and legislators were alerted to the troubles that were coming up fast, since the larger waves of students moving up the educational ladder were clearly about to descend on the university.[17] In that year, a ten-year "Fanfani" school development plan was proposed. After three or four years of discussion in the two legislative houses it became in 1962 a limited three-year plan devoid of any provision for structural reform of the university. A novel committee of inquiry established at that time came back with a report two years later, accompanied by a report from the minister of public instruction on guidelines for future development, out of which came a major university reform bill (No. 2314) which was endlessly debated during the middle 1960s and then came to naught.[18] The defeat of almost all portions of that bill was characterized by one deputy as another instance of academic power winning over political power. And a leading educational writer saw "the tortuous route" of No. 2314 as a repeat of the uncertainties and mistakes of "the political class" in respect to higher education during the twenty years since World War II.[19] Comma by comma, there had been a first-class political struggle: national associations representing students, assistants, and the nontenured professors battled openly for reform, while the chairholders' association fought against the changes and won. The proposed legislation included the establishment of departments and the outlawing of such "incompatibilities" as a professor's serving in Parliament while holding a chair. Neither change got through, nor did any provisions dealing with greater participation by junior faculty and students.

By 1968, after ten years of effort, it was clear that global legislation—sweeping reform—brought out too much opposition from the professors as well as the disapproval of one or another political party or party faction within the coalition government whose interests were touched adversely by some of the numerous provisions of a big bill. Those who have reviewed the legislation record since unification a century ago have pointed out that the Italian government has never passed major university reform bills other than under the authoritarian Fascist regime of 1922–43.[20] Even at the height of student protests during 1968 and 1969, conditions were still not appropriate for the grand proposal, for anything of the magnitude of the Edgar Faure reform law in France, passed under De Gaulle in 1968, which promised sweeping change. The Italians were in no position to enact the great plan that would capture the imagination of the nation and inform the world that they were seriously at work reforming an inadequate system.

"Small Laws"

However, the reformers did begin, in 1969, to obtain the passage of what were called "small laws" (*leggine*). Though the process vexed those who wanted numerous connected changes made at one time, either for ideological reasons of smashing the old structure or from a sense that so much needed to be coherently and quickly done, the *leggine* slipped through and began to chip away at the old. Something had to be done at the height of the student protest, and two changes enacted in 1969 responded to the claims that the university was undemocratic in access and rigid in the rites of passage. Access was "liberalized" by removing the restrictions that had kept the graduates of the less noble secondary schools, such as technical schools, from entering certain faculties, such as law and medicine. Now every person with a high school diploma could enter any university, any faculty, widening opportunity particularly for those from lower social strata who had been tracked into less prestigious secondary schools. Enrollment jumped by about 100,000 the following year (from about 650,000 in 1969–70 to more than 750,000 in 1970–71), increasing overload all along the line and especially in such a prized field as medicine.[21] A great pressure, backed by the unions and moderate-to-left political parties, had been responded to, without changing university organization or altering basic powers but at a cost of less control over input and more swamping of personnel and facilities.

A second change gave the students the right to ask for an individual program of study (*piano di studio*) and abolished the old distinction between fundamental and complementary courses, striking directly at the mandated courses that had been the heart of the national curriculum since the Fascist period. At a minimum, this change seemed to end the formal nationalization of curriculum in Italy, although informal and quasi-formal agreement among the faculties and chairs of a field might still enforce national uniformity, and professional associations retained the power to have their own requirements stating what is appropriate preparation at the university. At a maximum, the change considerably enlarged individual choice and greatly decentralized curriculum-making: Students could ask for individual programs, and faculties, faced by the necessity of dealing with individual programming, could work up their own sets of alternative requirements, often a common base of courses followed by optional tracks. Obviously this change also increased the overload of the operating structure: old fixed requirements were replaced by local bargaining between students, who by national law were granted a right to individual programs, and faculty members, who had their own sense of appropriate sets of courses.

Such changes continued in the early 1970s, with the most important ones altering the crucial examination system. A few fields such as engineering had had an examination that screened students at the end of the first two years of study. This "biannual" was eliminated as part of the continuing loosening of requirements. Then the general procedure for oral examination in each course was loosened. Traditionally, the student had to obtain from his faculty two months in advance a paper (*statino*) that admitted him to the examination and upon which the examiner wrote down the result, including failure. Now that infamous piece of paper was replaced by a system in which the student registered for and went to the examination. If he passed, that was written down; if he failed, no record was kept. This move largely eliminated the old distinction between regularly enrolled students and those in an out-of-course status (*fuori corso*); now all students had indefinite time for getting through.

This change also helped to ensure that more than ever before the examining of students would be the essential duty of the teaching personnel. Not only were there many more students to be tested, but, with liberalization in the taking of examinations, students would need to be examined more times as they kept coming back. "Sheer madness" was a common judgment on this change from within as well as from outside of the system: a "rational" planner could lose his mind just thinking about it. Why did "they" not substitute mass *written* testing for individual oral examination? They did not; no interest group chose this alternative and it never entered the debate. The only answer was to expand the three annual examination periods until examining was practiced virtually every month other than the sacred vacation month of August. The June examination became stretched from April through July; the fall period from September to November; and the third period from December to March. Even the nomenclature of the examination period became a virtual caricature of an examination "system" out of control. The June period consisted of a "Pre-appello" block of time in April and May, a "Primo appello" in June, a "Secondo appello" at the end of June, and a "Post appello" in July; and the student who did not pass in an early sitting was free to try again in a second subperiod within the same examination period. A similar structure held in the other two major examination periods.

Each day of examination in a major faculty became a test of manipulatory skills. The professor and his assistants, facing hordes, had to seek shortcuts while testing from morning to night. Examiners would spell one another; individual examinations would become ten minutes in length; more assistants would be called in to help out, including those who normally worked full time elsewhere. The students, now more anonymous in the mass and lost in a crush, had to seek ways of getting favorable treatment. They would seek to schedule a later appearance so as to learn the questions asked of those who appeared before them. They would attempt to be in the room when the mood was best: an early sitting, if the examiners were likely to be easier when less fatigued; a late one, if the examiners gave shorter exams when tired and anxious to be done. With space a problem, many examinations might be held simultaneously in one room, a bullpen of examiners and examinees, with others wandering around and listening in, since the oral examination was public and now many students had a sharpened interest in being a part of the listening public.

Thus, the reform in the examination system gave the student more leeway, first in scheduling when to be examined and second in coming back repeatedly in a persistent effort to pass. But if the examiners could no longer formally fail a student and stop him from coming back, they also did not have to pass him. In place of the old autocracy there was a somewhat more equal relation between examiners and students which had at times the flavor of a stand-off in endurance, with finally either the examiner cracking from fatigue and the need to expedite the work or the student giving up from discouragement. In general, by seeking to reduce the arbitrariness of the old system and to give the students greater opportunity for getting through, the reform accentuated the central place of examinations in the work of the system and added greatly to the examination overload.

Changes in Chair Power

The fall of 1973 (where our account ends) saw a fascinating legislative performance by the Italian government that cut somewhat closer to the bone than had the previous *leggine*. At the end of the summer, before professors, legislators, and other interested parties were fully reassembled from the mountains and the seashore, the government acted quickly to give higher education for a brief time the first order of priority. Instead of following the normal route of legislative action with all of its extensive consultation and long debate, the government issued an emergency decree (*decreto legge*) that had the standing of enacted law if not rolled back by the legislature acting decisively against it within sixty days—in this case, October 1 to November 30. In essence, this arbitrary action presented radical reformers and professors alike with a fait accompli: No effective countermove was mustered, and the decree became law.[22]

The most striking provision of the law was the projected creation of 7,500 new chairs for full professors, at the rate of 2,500 a year for three years, lifting the total number in the system from about 3,000 to more than 10,000.[23] There was little doubt about the potential significance of this authorization. If and when implemented, it would affect traditional power relations. At the operating level of the chair, power would be even more fractured since it would be distributed in three times as many sites. As junior staff were promoted rapidly to fill the *nuovi posti*, much new blood would flow into the chair level, at a rate not calculated to ensure dependable assimilation of the new to the old. Horizontal ties among chairs would have to change considerably; new faces in large numbers would intrude into the old connections that had been worked out carefully and stabilized over a long period of time. Here was promised expansion at the level of senior personnel that would be commensurate with the expansions that had already occurred in junior staff and students. Any change in size that was of the magnitude promised would considerably dilute the elite status accorded to the position when it was only for the few. In place of abolishing the position of chair—the direct attack desired by many—the decree seemed to endorse studied indirection as the means to weaken the power of existing chairholders. More people at the senior level in any sector of work at a university would lead toward multiperson decision-making, toward something like the interaction of senior professors in a department, even if departments were not established.

Second, the 1973 law tampered with the method by which persons were selected for chairs.[24] A few years earlier, the government had begun to intrude into this crucial area of decision-making, in which favoritism was so rampant, by suspending the *concorsi*—the national "competitions" for chairs—for a year. In a confusing manner, the *concorsi* suspension was maintained in several following years. The 1973 decree brought back the *concorsi* but also replaced the old system of electing the committee members who judged the competition; in the new method the judges would be selected by lottery from a relevant population of chairholders and nonchairholders. Drawing the commissioners by lot would negate much of the intense electoral politics of the old process that lay at the heart of national academic oligarchy. However, the retention of the *concorsi* maintained an important role for the national system qua system, vis-à-vis the individual university and faculty, since centrally operated committees would still decide who would be admitted to the charmed circle.

Third, the new law contained several provisions that aimed at stabilizing the position of the teaching ranks nearest to the chair professors and increasing their participation and power. Earlier, in 1966, a small stratum (three to four hundred) of near-professors (*professori aggregati*) had been created ad hoc. The new law eliminated this rank by folding its members into the chairholding group—a "stabilization" fervently desired by those in the category.[25] In addition, that large stratum we have so often mentioned —*professori incaricati*—was stabilized by being granted tenure firmly based in law and civil service.[26] They now would possess a status somewhat similar to that of the tenured associate professor in the United States. And from this more secure base, they would be able to exercise a greater voice. There was no doubt about implementation here, since no local action was required. The stabilization of this stratum fell within a typical Italian pattern of personnel expansion: with little or no legal authorization, add marginal personnel to help out in the work; then expand their numbers and provide minimal legal recognition; and finally fully institutionalize a stratum with laws that provide broad recognition and basic security and spell out rights and privileges. The belated recognition of these near-professors responded to the great discontent swelling within a stratum that absorbed much of the teaching load created by expansion. They could no longer be treated as helpers on year-to-year hire.

Another article in the law provided that these stabilized *incaricati* would now have greater rights of participation in the decision-making of local academic bodies.[27] They were to be full members of the councils that rule the faculties (*Consigli di Facoltà*), for everything other than decisions on chairs—an operating procedure that follows the logic, common in the United States, of not voting on the filling of ranks higher than one's own. This "participation" article called also for more representation of the *assistenti* in the Faculty Council. Similarly, provision was made to include members of groups other than that of chair professors, including students, in the administrative council of the whole university. Only time will tell how these measures will be attended to in the faculties and universities throughout the country. Without doubt they will be implemented unevenly. Yet overall, incremental gains in participation were being realized.

The 1973 law reflected a sense that the Italian university had to be on the agenda of the Italian government, if only for a day. The professors did not make the myriad marginal adjustments locally and nationally that might have kept the system viable. Other forces became impatient, then exasperated and inclined to act to break the logjam: the parties of the political center; the government in its highest councils; the unions, then growing more interested in a wide range of social issues and more powerful in their influence on government. What was done was done hastily and, in the eyes of Italian observers, was full of contradictions. Yet, even if it was full of compromise steps compared to the big reform ideas so extensively discussed throughout the 1960s, this government action still represented a defeat for the higher education establishment.

Creation of New Universities

The early 1970s saw another set of efforts that would likely prove increasingly important in the system: the creation of new universities. For the first time in the post-1945 period, including the hectic expansionist days of the late 1960s, the Italian government itself initiated a new university. In the fall of 1972 it created the University of Calabria. Placed in the south at the toe of the peninsula, the new university happened to fit certain political needs—different favors for different cities—as well as educational needs in one of the poorest sections of the country. It was sponsored and carried through the legislature by a powerful senator. Here, finally, was the kind of visible new start that allowed Italians to respond to questions about "innovation" by pointing to an organization new from the ground up—buildings, staff, students, curriculum, and all. Whether the university would be distinctive or conform to older patterns remained to be seen, but at least the national center showed some capacity to add new units to Italian higher education. The intention to do so was further reflected in an article of the 1973 law which pledged plans in the near future for the initiation of new universities, plans that were supposed to take into account the wishes of the regions as well as the ideas of central planning agencies concerning regional imbalance and priorities.[28]

A singularly dynamic force in the creation of new schools was the expanded use by local and provincial officials of an old pattern: under local sponsorship and financing, to start a faculty or university branch or even a university and then, in a few years, have it legally ratified and fully credited by lobbying it into the national system. The first center of sociological studies, in the form of a detached institute, was created in the 1960s in this fashion by conservative Christian Democrats in Trento. (However, shortly after the new unit was recognized as a part of the national system in 1966, its creators found to their horror that they had on their hands a center of student protest that drew militant radicals from Germany and other countries as well as from throughout Italy.)[29] Others took to this technique of initiation, which coincided with the growing interest throughout Italy in greater regionalization of governmental services and hence greater regional initiative and responsibility. As an example, a university site offering work in economics and commerce, teaching, and medicine was started in Verona as a branch of the University of Padua, and grew to more than 7,000 students by 1970.[30] With the country now moving into multibranch universities, the national system in 1970 could claim more than forty geographic sites and more than sixty recognized academic establishments, state and "free."[31] By 1973, there was talk of regional systems; a cluster of places east of Milan—Brescia, Bergamo, and Piacenza—was underway, and a half-dozen cities and towns around Turin wanted to have universities. In the center of Italy, where aside from the University of Rome there had been only extremely marginal universities, the University of Chieti, with its campuses at Chieti, Teramo, and Pescara under a common budget, was becoming considerably stronger, operating in effect as a regional subsystem within the national system. Cities too became more inclined to contribute financially to the support of faculties, old or newly established, that seemed relevant to their own needs: for example, teaching, at Ferrara; and economics and commerce, at Modena.

The new places have usually imitated the old ones, but their creation has allowed more room for new ideas and has at least extended geographic access. The recent proliferation of units shows that in actual operation the Italian *national* system is in a poor position to block local and provincial initiative. The places that have sprung up commonly have had the backing of local political forces, usually from within the ranks of the many factions of the long-dominant Christian Democrats, and both the national Christian Democratic party and the national planning office seemed willing to allow, even to encourage, this local sponsorship. With the cities moving into more cost-sharing with the national government, for some faculties a new dynamic of localism and regionalism seems to be emerging—a de facto regionalism that might well outstrip a de jure regionalization of the national set of universities.

Estimated Effects of the Reforms

Thus, as Italy moved into the mid-1970s, there were indications that the dam was breaking, that the chairholders, even if all 3,000 of them tried to plug the dike, could not hold back the flood-waters of pent-up demands for change. They could not stop numerical expansion of students and junior staff; nor the beginning of a break-up of the national curriculum; nor the initiation of new schools; nor, finally, efforts to dilute their individual power by expansion of their numbers and by increased participation of lower ranks.

But if our earlier analysis revealed anything it is that the Italian professors are not without capacity to make countermoves and to dilute any reform forced upon them. They will continue to hold much power, especially in the central faculties. They will continue to influence heavily the selection of new chairholders. In some cases, expansion will make the established chairholders stronger. If they install faithful followers in new chairs, they will extend and solidify the power of present clusters for the next two or three decades. They can also slow down or block the implementation of new laws: They can decide in a given faculty *not* to ask for any of the new chairs; they can be inhospitable to any *concorso* winner to the point where, in effect, he is not invited to the faculty; and they can find students' choices of courses of study lacking in merit and not approve them. As usual, actual practice will be negotiated, and the chairholding professor will still hold the greatest power in negotiation.

Still, the direction of change is toward reduction in the amount of power possessed by chairholders, individually and in small groups. First, there will be many more of them. And many new chairholders will use the turbulence of a period of crisis, overload, and ambiguity to free themselves considerably from the dominance of established *baroni* and *superbaroni*. Finally, the better-secured lower ranks will be less subject to the leverage of men in the rank above them.

Most important in estimating long-run effects of reform are the ways in which the changes of the 1960s and early 1970s heightened or diminished the fundamental features of the entire system of Italian higher education. We have emphasized a traditional double balkanization in the system—higher education as a sector of government considerably autonomous of other sectors and fragmented into several hundred faculties and several thousand chairs and institutes that possess surprising degrees of autonomy. The recent changes increase rather than decrease this internal fragmentation: for example, 10,000 chairs will replace 3,000. Fragmentation is also increased by the proliferation of branches and new units in one city after another.

However, this fragmentation will not go unopposed. The principal formal tool of administrative unity, the administrative director and his staff at each university, has been increasingly developed since 1960 as a more active systematizer of university life. Based in "the business side" of university activities, a growing full-time administrative class, in Italian universities as elsewhere, is bound to become indispensable to the amateur administrators who are supposed to run the academic side. In organizations that have grown greatly in size and complexity, the administrative directors are the ones who have the requisite knowledge and expertise as well as the formal responsibility of obeying national, legally sanctioned administration. And since administration at the level of university-wide and faculty-wide organization has become one of the most glaring weaknesses of the Italian system—a weakness that encouraged chairholders to be arbitrary—we may anticipate efforts to increase coordination on the academic side by strengthening the offices of university rector and faculty dean. This strengthening, which is already underway in other Continental countries, means such changes as lengthened terms of office for rectors and deans; greater weight given to administrative ability in selection of these officeholders; greater influence by higher levels of administration, including, possibly, appointment from above in place of election by peers; and a strengthening of the immediate staff of these principal academic heads. The overload of traditional structure that has taken place will not much longer allow these positions to go untouched, and academicians can respond effectively to the growing role of the administrative directors only by strengthening their own bureaucratic capacity.

We have also underlined the high degree to which the Italian national structure of higher education is a politicized system. The environment of reform is thus neither a market in which organizations competitively adjust to changing conditions nor a bureaucracy in which managers consciously adjust organization to new demands. Some planning will develop and a little competition might even spring up, but neither is a primary force. The basic environment is that of patrimonial politics, intensely political behavior within a particularistic hierarchy of professional power that happens to be lodged within the framework of a national agency. The implementation of reform is therefore not a matter of bureaucratic directives nor of professional injunctions but of efforts that must be intensively political in nature. To affect the system, reform must first of all affect its political components. When the professors attempted to ward off all reforms that would challenge the traditional structures, using every political weapon in their considerable arsenal to maintain the status quo, they were ensuring that, in time, it would be politics that would be turned against them. There were no other tools. The only course left was a shift from internal politics to the politics of the larger arena, where the interests of other powerful groups would, in time, be heightened and coalesce more frequently in a mood of intervention.

Put only a little differently, neither elegant educational logic nor a search for greater effectiveness was here the way to purposive change. In public administration, as Harold Seidman has put it, "economy and efficiency are demonstrably not the prime purposes."[32] Rather, the basic issues relate to power: who shall control it and to what ends? In the higher education sector of the Italian government, the senior academics have controlled power to the end of protecting their individual and collective welfare; thus the breaking of *that* power in the service of *those* ends is what reform is about. The efforts to reform and the reforms themselves attempt to spread power to more academic personnel and to more external groups. If the political dimensions of the system are changed, then the ends of other groups may be partially serviced and countervailing forces may be established that will open the system to greater influence of universal standards and objective judgments.

Because the political dimensions are so basic—an extreme case of a common phenomenon—reform is not a matter of global planning but of adjustment through (1) political incrementalism, (2) studied indirection, and (3) negotiated planning. Everywhere in complex organizations, for reasons best explained by Charles E. Lindblom, marginal adjustment is a common administrative necessity and style.[33] Under reasonably unitary authority, chief executives use their administrative judgment to make the more impelling adjustments, coolly weighing the gains and losses. In a setting of dispersed authority, such adjustments fall to political negotiation, with such political activities as bargaining amounting to decision-making through mutual adjustment.[34] The structure of the Italian subgovernment for higher education, and Italian government in general, pushes action strongly in this direction, forcing the negotiation of minor adjustments. An aspect of this incrementalism is a capacity to work out of "crises" time and again by marginal adjustments that provide sufficient equilibrium to keep things going.

In such a setting, reform efforts are often heavily characterized by studied indirection.[35] It simply does not make sense to work out an open, comprehensive attack, despite the advantages of coherently linking changes, if the sweeping effort will rip apart a weak association of disparate groups. Piecemeal, gradual change safeguards a precarious consensus by avoiding the radical attack that is sure to increase conflict. Given the typical structure of academic organizations as amalgams of disciplines, it is perhaps not a result of timid character that the agents of academic reform so often resort to attack by small and glancing blows rather than by unambiguous frontal assaults. In Italian higher education, studied indirection is a way of life, and it is almost always essential to the maintenance of the system. And so it is also in the highest councils of government, where the safeguarding of precarious coalition is the first order of the day.

In this setting, effective planning has to be negotiated planning or planned bargaining (*contrattazione programmata*), as it has become known in relations between Italian government and Italian industry.[36] If one party cannot compel another to follow a plan, it can consult and bargain and move ahead where limited agreement is possible. Given the cellular construction of the university system, it is difficult to compel action: effective power remains in hundreds and thousands of places in the countryside, in the hands of experienced academics schooled in mutual adjustment. When we recall that the professor, as senior administrator of a domain, implements what he helped to determine as senior politician in the encompassing academic polities, it becomes clear that planners must of necessity move ahead by a steady process of negotiation.

One final item in the equations of reform is the weakness of central political authority at the top of the Italian government.[37] Coalition government in Italy since the Fascist period has been the weakest of those in the large democratic countries in Western Europe. In a country that has sought to centralize authority *and* administration, the democratic regimes have been unable to establish a strong, top decision-making center in Rome. This favors the internal balkanizing of government that we have highlighted as well as the strengthening of power centers outside the government; the two often go hand in hand, as the internal group allies itself with an external faction. Thus, what has actually developed is a combination of weak centralized *authority* in control of broad public policy and strong centralized *organization* in the sense of powerful sectors that manage the activities for which the government has formally taken responsibility. The form of sectoral control can vary from bureaucratic dominance to a capture of power by an external or internal group other than the administrative class. With the latter happening in Italian higher education, it has been difficult for central political authorities to intrude for at least three major reasons: (1) based upon unsteady coalition, they deal from a shaky position; (2) their tool of intervention is a low-quality, weak civil service; and (3) they risk reaction from an interest group, the professoriate, whose power is deeply entrenched in the implementing bureau and elsewhere in the government. Also, in the face of shifting priorities among all the important problems it faces, the government's attention span is necessarily short. It is fully preoccupied with urgent considerations of foreign policy, industrial incentives, monetary stability, control of civic violence, the development of the south, and indeed the strengthening of the capacity of the government itself at the very top to handle the pressing agenda of modern government in a credible way. In the field of social services, there is much to be done in reform of hospitals, prisons, pensions—and every other service sector administered by a bureau. When "the government," at a level above the ministry, attends to higher education, it is likely to intervene only in fits and starts. It moves only when it has to, in order to survive the pressure of complaints of aggrieved and discontented factions within and outside this sector. Most of the time, it is inclined to avert its eyes, to follow Machiavelli's injunction that "the wiser course is to temporize." When the government does occasionally intervene, it is itself likely to move by studied indirection.

And what of the long run? Given that a particular traditional form of power monopolization has become increasingly the prime defect of the Italian system, the drift of interventions will be to erode that national network of academic power. Various systems are impelled in different directions in reform under the impact of modern demands: the Italian system requires reaction in the form of decentralizing and deconcentrating power. Whatever the dangers of increased inequity and local parochialism, the long-run drift will inevitably be toward more regional and local responsibility in higher education which will foreshorten the reach of academic oligarchy.

Reform in Cross-national Perspective

Wherever systems of higher education are evolving from an elite conception to mass involvement, the new demands of student expansion, staff expansion, and knowledge specialization, accompanied by shift in attitudes toward democratization and participation, will render problematic the existing coordinating structure. The demands themselves will vary in impact according to the nature of the existing system and will hit hardest at formally monolithic, nationalized systems, and especially those controlled internally by academic oligarchs. This is because the new demands run strictly in the contrary direction, toward heterogeneity of structure and control. They press for institutional variety in the form of many types of colleges and universities, for example, technical institutes, colleges of advanced technology, independent research centers, short-cycle comprehensive colleges, quasi-autonomous research centers within universities, teachers' colleges, regional colleges, elite universities *and* mass universities. They seek a proliferation, even a vast confusion of degree levels and programs, contrary to the logic of uniformity, of minimal differentiation, that is deeply embedded in the formal structures and processes of the unitary system. The heterogeneity of clientele, employment connections, and fields of knowledge incorporated in mass higher education also presses for a separation, covert if not overt, of personnel who deal with necessary "elite" functions from those who, like public secondary-school teachers, must face the general public.

In *relative* ease of adjusting higher education to modern pressures, the United States seems to rank at one end, Great Britain, West Germany, and France in a middle group, and Italy at the other end. The American system is marked by historically given heterogeneity, permitting adaptations in various and even contradictory directions. Already selective colleges have become even more selective, at the same time that the rapid proliferation of short-cycle units in the form of community colleges has opened the door unselectively to mass involvement. Although the public sector is ever more dominant in quantity and has impressive quality at the top, the private sector retains much prestige and allows institutional identities that are contrary to the mainstream. The traditional diverse structure, especially the multiple forms of control, has allowed much ad hoc, incremental, and divergent adjustment. Both the market and planning are at work.

The British system is more unified than the American; it is considerably smaller in number of institutions and overall size, and it is considerably integrated by tacit agreement within a much smaller intellectual elite, many of whose members have been educated in just two universities.[38] The University Grants Committee has long operated as a national body distributing funds from one major source. Market mechanisms are diminished and state planning enhanced. But the system has not been monolithic to the point where traditional academic oligarchs could prevent the national government from supporting the growth of new universities and enlarging the nonuniversity sectors. There have been a number of institutional types: Oxford-Cambridge; the University of London, operating uniquely as a country-wide and partially worldwide academic holding company; provincial universities; technological universities; and teacher-training colleges.[39] British higher education underwent extensive structural alteration in the 1960s: in the university sector alone, ten entirely new universities were created and a somewhat larger number of existing institutions were "raised" to university status.[40] And, in the early 1970s, the Open University entered the field as a British solution for delayed and recurrent higher education.

The German federal structure has given the different *Länder* the authority and the organizational leeway to experiment in a number of directions, including the creation of new units in the university sector, such as Aachen and Bochum in the Nordrhein-Westfalen Land, and Konstanz in the Baden-Württemberg Land.[41] Manpower suction plays a more dynamic role in Germany than in France and Italy, since the German university has been better connected to industry, with the needs of the industrial sector influencing technology and science at the university.[42] But the features of the German structure that tend to open it to change face strong contrary tendencies: the imposing traditional power of the academic notable, perhaps even greater than that observed in Italy, since organization of the chair and institute is tighter and more efficient; the suppression of pragmatic adjustment by incorporation of specific issues into broad ideological conflict that produces stalemate; and the great pains devoted to the legalistic definition of what must be done, what may be done, and what ought not be done.

In the French system, as in the Italian case, formal adjustments in different directions by different parts of the system have not normally been possible; few interest groups of any power have pressed for structural differentiation. A proposed change for any part of the system must be raised to the level of national debate, there to be subsumed under broad ideologies. Overall, the structure is heavily resistant to adjustment. But, as noted earlier, the French system has been more infused than the Italian with a commitment to high standards, and it is also part of a government that possesses stronger planning capacity and greater political strength, independent of the professors, to intrude upon the academic system.[43] Thus it has been possible for the French to enunciate broad new plans in a time of crisis—for example, the De Gaulle-supported Faure reform of 1968—even if typically the reform bogs down in implementation. The 1968 reform actually effected such structural changes as the breaking up of the mammoth University of Paris into thirteen parts and the banishing of the Faculty as the secondary organizational level in the system.

The Italian system must be placed tentatively at the bottom of the list in *formal* adaptability because of the nature of the deeply entrenched structure of the system as it moved into the 1960s. With its structure held in comparative view, it is the changes of the recent years rather than the previous lack of change that are noteworthy. We have seen how and why the changes occurred, through crisis-related response to protest and overload and through processes over which no one had any possibility of control. But behind the zigzag course of surface events, behind even the "chaos" assigned by foreign observers to Italian civic life, the substructure of the system is remarkably persistent and likely to evolve only by bits and pieces, in incremental adjustment. Since so much about the substructure remains hidden as well as complexly interwoven, the Italian system of higher education is likely to remain relatively opaque to continuous assessment and easy predictability. When more is brought to light, the Italian system may prove to have a balance of forces favoring evolutionary change that would be on a par at least with those of France, Germany, and Britain. For example, general regional decentralization and the assertion of local initiative may be developing at a more rapid rate in Italy than in France, since Italy's centralization is less effectively rigid in resisting change, and its local notables, using such instruments as the political parties, are disposed increasingly to maneuver around the old, discredited state apparatus.[44] A guess is warranted that the higher education sector will be somewhat further caught up in the initiatives of the regions and the cities. At least, this is the best long-run hope for substantive change in the structure of Italian higher education.

To glance roughly as we have done at the distribution of academic power in other societies, from the vantage point of the Italian extreme, is to be struck anew by the tenacity of faculty-based organization. The task remains to clarify the stubborn organizational form that most undergirds individual and collective power of academic men.

Five

G U I L D

It is not a question of discovering whether the medieval institution can identically fit our contemporary societies, but whether the needs which it answered are not always present, although it must, in order to satisfy them, change according to the times.

Emile Durkheim, *The Division of Labor in Society*

By a frequently diffident attitude towards the public at-large the amalgam formed by groups and bureaucracy derives its characteristics of a counter-system to political democracy.... Objectively [the group leaders and administrators] may multiply states within the state and thereby reconstitute the technicalities of a feudal system.

Henry W. Ehrmann, "Interest Groups
and the Bureaucracy in Western Democracies,"
in Reinhard Bendix, ed., *State and Society*

It is striking that the great modern forms for the organization of work, bureaucracy and profession, intersect so much in the academic world with a supposedly medieval form that still finds place in the twentieth century. If in the beginning in Bologna there was the guild, functioning as a recognized form of local public-private authority within the loosely organized context of political and ecclesiastical control, so, today in Italy, after a century of national unification, two decades of Fascist centralization, and three decades of regularization of an educational administrative state, followed by the recent reforms, there remains the guild—professors in the organized work commune. At a time when power is increasingly likely to be concentrated in the state, the guild remains an important means of countervailing power in the hands of faculties.

In this chapter we will clarify the traditional meaning of guild and suggest its present potential for analysis with three specific intentions in mind: to connote in the term the organization of control that is at the heart of the striking features of the Italian case; to point to a wider phenomenon of professional influence inside the bureaus of government, of which state-employed academic personnel are a special and revealing case; and to suggest that a similar form of control is present in other national systems of higher education, although commonly more diluted by stronger application of other forms of control. If our reexamination of this term for its contemporary usefulness is persuasive, it should also help diminish the widespread impression that guild-like features are totally inappropriate in modern organization. As Emile Durkheim has pointed out, elements of medieval institutions need not be anachronistic. In modified form, they may still answer needs that are always present—for example, the efficacious regulation of an occupational activity, which cannot be done by the state or society but rather only "by a group intimate enough with it to know its functioning, feel all its needs, and able to follow all their variations."[1]

THE TRADITIONAL MODEL

As indicated in Chapter 1, the university began as a scholastic guild at a time when the guild was the basic form for the organization of work.[2] Guilds were associations of men "belonging to the same class, or engaged in kindred pursuits, or with certain common interests or aims, formed for mutual aid and protection."[3] They could be basically political, religious, social, or occupational, and often had a mixture of functions, but the principal types developed around trade and craft.[4] The guild has had great longevity, in Italy going back two thousand years into Roman times.[5] In its earlier stages, it was a first step outward from kinship, replacing the family as the framework for work and offering protection to those thus drawn together. It was a secondary group, but one with many primary-group characteristics, including familylike intimacy, with apprentices living with the family and under the personal control of the master-father.[6] In the craft guild, the personalized relations of a small social system became part of an association based on occupation and were there fused with ownership of the means of production and the control of labor [7]

The craft guilds attempted to establish autonomous and self-perpetuating control over a guild district, essentially a small monopoly over a type of work in a defined territory.[8] They limited access to work by controlling admission to membership, as in some modern professions and unions. They effected a vertical dimension of full and subordinate membership in strata of masters, journeymen, and apprentices, with each master personally supervising a small cluster of journeymen and apprentices. An apprentice had to serve a certain number of years before he might become a journeyman, and a journeyman had to produce a "masterpiece" before becoming a master.[9] Apprentices and journeymen were judged by the masters. Among themselves, masters were interested in equality: they exercised collective control by electing their own officials, and then, under guild oath, all were to obey the laws and rules enacted.[10] Thus at the senior level, authority was primarily horizontal, binding master to master in a body of equals.

The relation between guilds and public authorities varied widely through time and from one place to another. In some states, guilds were not even formally recognized, whereas in others guilds served directly as arms of government—despite the tendency in the literature to describe them as voluntary associations, a formulation that emphasizes independence. Max Weber speaks of an unfree type of guild closely controlled by the state, even initiated by it, that was found in late antiquity and in Egypt,

India, and China, with the free-association type developing later in Europe in the Middle Ages.[11] Sylvia Thrupp, concentrating on Western Europe, defines five phases of development "in each of which the relationship between small voluntary association and public authority changed."[12] The early guilds were for a time unchallenged by weak monarchies. But in later centuries monarchies, town governments, and state governments sought to control and use them for public ends. They became enmeshed in a system of state-regulated privileges, and thus were not allowed to retain their blissful state of independence as the quintessence of private voluntary association. Towns and states rendered them quasi-public.

Emergence of the Academic Guild

When *academic* guilds emerged as the first universities, they amounted to a discovery (or rediscovery) of organized group life in the pursuit of the highest teaching and learning:

> The underlying characteristics which distinguished the medieval university from all previous educational regimes was its corporatism. Unlike the monastic scholar, who often studied in isolation, the university masters and students invariably worked as a group. Following the pattern of the trade and craft guild, they sought to organize themselves for regulation of the conditions vital to their profession. Chief among these was exclusive admission to membership, and the universities guarded this privilege with hypersensitivity.[13]

Control over membership was as important in the new students' associations as in the masters': "Like the guild, the Bolognese law students bound themselves with an oath, swore obedience to elected officials, and closely regulated admission to their membership."[14]

Within the self-regulating faculty groups, the internal hierarchy—right down to certain titles—came from the guild model:

> At the bottom were the ordinary students, equivalent to the guild apprentices who were learning the elements of the trade and were under the full authority of the master craftsmen. Next came the bachelors, who were advanced students and were allowed to lecture and dispute under supervision. They corresponded to and derived their names from the journeymen or bachelors, who worked for a daily wage and

had not sufficient maturity to establish themselves in the trade. (Hence they were still unmarried.) At the top of the profession was the master, a rank common to both universities and guilds. He was a man who had demonstrated both his skill and maturity to the satisfaction of his fellow masters. Entrance to this stage was gained after elaborate examinations, exercises in the techniques of teaching, and ceremonial investiture.[15]

Although the student guild in Bologna was the dominant body for several centuries, "the masters always had a college of their own, to which alone belonged the right of admitting new masters or (in the modern phrase) 'granting degrees'."[16] Thus the Bologna model was a two-tier guild system, with the faculty holding control over admission to the upper level. When the Italian student organizations weakened after the fourteenth century, the two tiers became one, as elsewhere in Europe, converging in the single internal hierarchy of control described above. The top rank of master was even then known as professor: "The three titles, master, doctor, professor, were in the Middle Ages absolutely synonymous."[17]

The guild organization of trade and industry, rooted in locality, was greatly diminished in the seventeenth to nineteenth centuries, under the impact of the entrepreneur, the factory, and the extended market. Marx portrayed its complete disappearance: "All in all, the entire gild system—both master and journeyman—dies out, when the capitalist and the labourer emerge"; the patriarchal relationship between journeyman and master was replaced "by the monetary relation between worker and capitalist."[18] And at the end of the nineteenth century Durkheim was troubled that the guild had not been sufficiently supple to reform and maintain itself, since its decline made for weakness in occupational groupings that mediated between the individual and the state. Therefore, Western society "after a century of groping and fruitless experience," was left in need of a revived and modernized version of what had existed before.[19] However, elements of guild mentality, if not guild forms, remained in the economic sector, within the craft unions and the professional associations that developed more strongly after the time of Durkheim.[20]

For the academic world, we can be fairly sure of what lies in the gaps of missing history. The spirit of capitalism was not to reign in academia: there were no profit-seeking entrepreneurs building factories, hiring wage laborers, and producing for extended markets. The guild form was not thrust into "a competitive structure in which it has to be better than alternative forms of organization in order to survive."[21] That reason alone would have been enough to carry the form forward in history. Thus, despite occasional heavy-handed intervention by church and state, faculty clusters retained guild principles of organization at the operating levels of academic work with remarkable persistence and unbroken continuity.[22] From the twelfth to the twentieth century, the university has predominantly had the shape of a federation of guilds.[23] Historically, the guild is *the* generic organizational form for the support of academic work.

Essence of Guild Organization

What are the essential characteristics of this organizational form? Certain features that have been absent at different times and places can be eliminated from consideration. We noted above that guild units need not be voluntary associations in the private sector; they have often been under tight state supervision, holding quasi-public status. It is also not essential that such specific patterns as the taking of a guild oath be maintained; this medieval practice became truly anachronistic in later settings. Similarly, the injunction to obey elected officials was not the moral imperative in later centuries that it was in the twelfth: in the earlier period hierarchical obedience was assumed to be necessary for establishing order. The patterns of familylike relations were not always strong or necessary. Guild organization has leeway for particular personal ties and can readily induce paternalism, but it need not be a closed vessel of intimacy: students need not live with the professor; junior teaching staff need not remain unmarried; and professors need not think of their faculty as a fraternity.

The essence of guild lies in a combination of autocratic and collegial control; it is an organizational form that combines personal rulership with collegiate rulership.[24] Autocratic control is found in the domain of the master. There, in the primary unit, strong vertical control involves personal supervision over a small district of work and subordinate staff and learners. Collegial control obtains in the domain of a group of masters. There, strong horizontal linkage entails group supervision over a larger work district and a larger body of subordinates. The guild thus combines autocrats and colleagues. It so divides and shapes authority that autocracy can exist within a collegial group and collegiality among autocrats. The idea of the guild has long meant the linkage of these vertical and horizontal patterns, and continues to do so. Some observers remark only on the collegial parts, applying the term "guild" to collective control of a domain of work or, in the academic world, to a "community of scholars."[25] Others emphasize the vertical component, applying "guild" to personal hegemony of the superior over subordinates. But a minimal analytical conception must note the presence and coupling of the two components.

In actuality, the elements of vertical and horizontal control vary in degree. A high degree of both constitutes "pure guild." When autocratic rule is relatively weak and collegial control remains strong, the control structure will be most noteworthy for peer dominance. A group of masters without subordinates would be the extreme case, and historically many faculty clusters have come close to this form when there were only a few assistants and students, on the average, for each professor. In contrast, when autocratic control is strong and collegial rule is weak, personal authority will rule the scene. Many Italian faculties have exhibited this pattern, in which professors can be arbitrary in their own domains, with only pro forma efforts at collective control. Finally, when autocracy and collegiality are both weak, guild organization suffers and is vulnerable to dominance by other forms.

Causes of Guild Survival

If guild organization persisted in academic work because, in part, it did not encounter sharp competition from other forms of organization, it would also have persisted because of the way faculty interests became vested in it and supporting ideologies worked out around it.[26] It matches particularly well the definition of the university as a self-governing community of scholars. Moreover, the guild may still effectively serve some of the most basic needs of academic life.

First, guild organization makes groups of experts collectively responsible for the maintenance of standards and the general quality of work in fields where a high degree of expertise renders nonexperts incapable of informed judgment. The university, as a conglomerate of such fields, greatly needs such on-the-spot collective responsibility.

Second, guild organization, by apprenticing neophytes and the partially trained, provides sensitive and prolonged socialization into advanced fields. Its vertical dimension of authority provides for training through personal relationships, a particularly relevant form whenever a specialty needs long training, close supervision, and much intuitive judgment. Since the university is a center of training for the highest competence in the most esoteric specialties, its professors readily assume the role of master in the effort to transmit the complexities of their knowledge and judgment.

Third, by permitting the immediate work group to determine how work is to be done and who is to do it, guild organization offers small faculty clusters considerable defense against the claims for control of other groups, particularly the authority of much larger and ultimately more powerful bodies, such as the state, which provide funding. It serves as a bulwark in the university for small-group autonomy in teaching, learning, and research. Moreover, it provides for some individual autonomy within the group; in the nineteenth and twentieth centuries, faculty groups, in pursuing the ideals of freedom of teaching and research, increasingly granted much autonomy to the individual master.

To push the argument on the functions of the academic guild to its limit, we might say that no university to date has been great without considerable guild authority at the levels where teaching and research actually take place. If aspects of the guild did not exist within the modern university, they would have to be invented.

Wherever advanced specialties exist, as in the professions, some of the old habits of the guild are maintained: group control of entry and certification; dominion of the fully certified over subordinates; and peer review and collective decision-making in work practice. At root, the guild is a "rational" form because of the need to center governance around expertise. That need is multiplied in the academic world since the occupation as a whole contains numerous and diverse specialties ranging across the humanities, the social sciences, the physical and biological sciences, and the professional schools. The academic profession is a holding company of disciplines and professions. But it is fractured rather than united by specialism. Primary membership is in the specialties—psychology, English, physics, law—not in the university. Therefore the form of organization most fitting at the operating level is not unitary bureaucracy or unified profession. It is necessarily some version of the guild, with a heavy degree of collective authority granted to experts, within and among a large number of small cells, and, within the cells, some hierarchical placement of expertise analogous to that of master, journeyman, and apprentice.

THE MODERN MIXTURE OF GUILD, BUREAUCRACY, AND PROFESSION

Naturally, guild characteristics do not stand alone in the university. They are surrounded and penetrated by other major forms of organization, especially bureaucracy, which has everywhere been strengthened by the search for administrative order in ever larger and more complex systems.

Guild versus Bureaucracy

In pure version, bureaucracy is the antithesis of guild, offering downward control and upward accountability in a pyramid of formal positions, with no provision for personal control and collegial rights. Bureaucracy moves into prominence as higher education becomes a governmental agency and takes up a niche within the vast network of large bureaus that constitute modern public administration. With the university increasingly placed inside government, especially in national systems but also in state and provincial systems, the guildlike faculty clusters that have long mediated the relation of academic worker and the state become an organizational part of the state. The master takes up the role of state official, having the formal status of a civil servant and becoming the recognized head of a segment of a bureau. In this dual status, the professor is pushed and pulled between several forms of control.[27]

It is often assumed that as modern structures of higher education become parts of centralized national bureaucracies they must necessarily succumb to the bureaucratic form, and that faculties and professors must lose their autonomy. But this is not always the case. Any analysis of where power lies in the system, any judgment on whether autonomy is being gained or lost, depends not so much on whether the university is formally a part of the state but rather on the relative strength of the historically rooted forms of organization characteristic of each. In the conflict between such major forms of organization as bureaucracy and guild, the relative power of these forms at a given time and place determines the nature of the accommodation. Thus, despite the great growth of bureaucratic patterns in formal organizations in the twentieth century, it is safe to say that no one is going to write the organizational history of the German, French, or British university systems—up to 1970 in any event—as a constant triumph of bureaucracy. Rather, the professors have continued to exercise considerable control while the state framework has had to adjust to the reality of their power.

Clearly, guild organization can serve as an effective power base for professors even when the universities are inside the government. As we have seen, in Italy the interests of senior professors, expressed through guild organization, are dominant. As a result, the state administrative structure for higher education is considerably balkanized. We have referred to double balkanization—the autonomy of parts of a bureau within an autonomous bureau. This double balkanization of the formal administrative structure serves as an accommodation of the bureaucracy to the guild. To understand why the balkanizing tendency is so strong and difficult to overcome, it is necessary to examine the persisting power of guild features of occupational life within modern organizations.

Guild and Professional Organization

Guild principles operative in modern organizations also must relate to professional principles. The concept of profession does not speak specifically to the organized ways in which local clusters of practitioners go about controlling their affairs, although the more realistic analyses of recent years have been moving in that direction. As discussed in Chapter 3, professions tend not to organize tightly for strong self-policing across their length and breadth, but leave much control to the many clusters that compose them. The local clusters thus turned loose seem often to be guildlike units that, in various combinations in different professions, combine hierarchical control by senior members over junior staff and horizontal collegiality among these seniors, this collegiality including collective authority in general policy and peer review in questions of appropriate practice and competence. In short, the operating units of professions make extensive use of guild principles of organization. This is bound to be most true in the academic profession, with its extremely loose overall organization qua profession and its pursuit of academic freedom and corresponding avoidance of inspector-generals.

As a member of a large occupational group, the local senior professor will find some congruence between guild and professional organization, but he is also likely to encounter tensions between local collegiality and the broader government of the profession. Again, the nature of an accommodation depends on the relative strength of aspects of each, as determined by historical primacy and depth of structural roots. In Italy, the great guildlike power of the local academic masters has weakened the pull of universal professionalism. The cells of monopoly power have balkanized not only the bureaucratic structure but also the professional framework; personal domination is widespread in local and regional parts of academic disciplines. Also, the Italian combination of guild and bureaucracy has made professional association the great loser. Guildlike organization at the bottom overlaid with a bureaucratic framework at the top seems to have reduced the play of professional association at middle levels of linkage whereby local disciplinary clusters are tied into regional and national organizations of disciplines. But whatever the outcome of this three-way interaction, the guild form, even if diminished to a minor role, is not likely to fade away entirely. It attends to small-scale arrangements within the large-scale systems; it provides for personal relations within classic forms of secondary organization; and it asserts direct democracy among peers while simultaneously it grades privilege in levels of competence.

We have also observed in Italy, along with the advantages of the guild form for academic work, the pitfalls, the disadvantages, of guild organization in modern academic systems. Like any other form, the guild can become too strong, radically diminishing features of bureaucracy and profession that perform useful functions. When guild operation amounts to a virtual monopoly of power, it precludes the organized expression of the interests of relevant external groups and the rights of individuals who cluster in subordinate sites within the system. It wards off external control through the defense provided by balkanized structure; it sees that no independent administration arises within the system; it grants individual professors and clusters of professors arbitrary authority over subordinates. Those who are served by its combination of autocracy and collegiality stretch its workings from the small settings of chair and faculty to the large setting of national system, so "guilding" the larger framework that national administration turns into a mock bureaucracy, a screen behind which operates the most intense personal politics. The guild form is then the tool of oligarchical particularism in the coordination of the whole national system. At this extreme, guild (and professional) ideals are debased; narrow self-interest triumphs over the maintenance of standards and the delivery of honest, dependable service.

Moreover, the generalist nature of the control of the local autocrat is antithetical to high quality in specialized work within modern disciplines. As the master-professor accumulates roles in the manner observed in Italy, he loses technical competence, as compared with that of the specialists, while simultaneously increasing his orientation to political and administrative matters. His choice of academic friends and assistants and his judgments about the worth of others are affected accordingly. Under these circumstances, collegial rulership, with its special processes of peer selection and supervision, tilts the whole structure away from objective judgment on the quality of specialists.

Also, guild forms have traditionally been a part of small-scale organization but now, when stretched as in Italy, are asked to serve effectively in modern large-scale settings, settings that include a much higher degree of specialization than obtained in the past. The proliferation of various specialist groupings within the collegial body has made it decidedly less cohesive and less willing or able to supervise the autocratic professor. The potential for inequality is enhanced. This is particularly true when the larger and more loosely joined guild is part of an administrative structure, for then those who hold basic power can write the bureaucratic rules and use them for their own advantage.

In short, unless the guild form is set in a frame of effective checks and balances with other forms of organization, it can so monopolize the control of higher education that it promotes excesses of arbitrary authority. This is the Italian problem.

The Guilding of Public Enterprise

In helping us to understand whether guild features of organization have useful functions or are merely anachronisms, the study of systems of higher education also helps to shed light on organizational development in other sectors of society, particularly those that increasingly fall within the broad realm of public administration. Though, as some have contended, guild forms may have largely disappeared in the work organization of private industry and in the general labor force of industrial and commercial activities (except in the labor force of certain crafts), in the academic sector, as we have shown, the situation has been fundamentally different. There, this age-old pattern has been retained—strongly in the chair-based systems that predominate around the world, and in more muted form in department-based systems. As individual universities are taken up within public systems, the small collectivities that historically have composed them move inside the general framework of provincial and national ministries and continue to exercise much authority. Seen in this light, academic groups have been in the forefront of professional groups that have seemingly been sucked into and under state control but have in fact developed considerable leverage in the use of "their" part of the state. The other professional groups have found features of guild organization to be congenial to the work of their craft as well as to the defense of their privileges. But only recently have observers noted the capacity of occupational groups to organize themselves within the house of government, sharing a consciousness of craft as well as constructing horizontal and vertical ties among experts that promote group control of a bureau.

We may thus view the public sector as increasingly occupied by small associations of allied professionals pursuing group self-interest (although to what ends that self-interest is connected is problematic). This means that representation by occupation operates heavily within the executive branch of government and in related committee systems of the legislature, even while overall representation in the legislature is still formally based on locality. As Gaetano Mosca has noted, in the past "the opposition of the part against the whole arose along local lines," while today that opposition "has a functional basis."[28] De facto government becomes government by occupational group, with control exercised from internal as well as external sites. Tucked away within that reality of modern political and organizational life lie the use and abuse of guild forms of association and control. In the latest stage of guild development, guildlike clusters appear primarily within the administrative machinery of the state. There, as so often in history, they still combine public and private ends.

Talcott Parsons may yet be right in his general proposition that "the massive emergence of the professional complex, not the special status of capitalistic or socialistic modes of organization, is the crucial structural development in twentieth-century society."[29] But if professionals are crucial it is because they combine power based on expertise with power based on group control of positions within government as well as in occupations located more strictly in the private sector. And with that development come no guarantees of detachment, universalism, and altruistic service; opposite outcomes are likely. The tilt depends on the combination of forms of organization within and around the professional group. The guild is one of the generic forms, exhibited in the extreme in Italian academic life.

THE ACADEMIC GUILD IN CROSS-NATIONAL PERSPECTIVE
Over a century ago, Matthew Arnold was sent to the Continent by a Schools Enquiry Commission of the British Government to study the educational systems of France, Italy, Germany, and Switzerland. Upon his return, he expressed the view that scholars were finally becoming aware of how much they could learn by comparative study of institutions, and he urged that we "treat this comparative study with proper respect, not to wrest it to the requirements of our inclinations or prejudices, but to try simply and seriously to find what it teaches us."[30]

On certain topics, not much has changed since Arnold's time: in the comparative analysis of academic power, the state of the art remains primitive, still at the stage where "we are at last beginning to see that much light can be thrown by leaving home."[31] Even rudimentary description of who does what to whom has been lacking for almost every country; ethnographic accounts or country case studies are needed if further light is to be thrown.[32] Current knowledge of academic organization has also remained deficient in categories that will help in the comparison of countries and in concepts that will help organize and summarize the descriptive materials. Appropriate concepts, however basic, will aid us in discovering "simply and seriously" what comparative study can teach us today.

We have refurbished the concept of guild authority not only to connote best the nature of academic power in Italy but also to help cast light on power in other academic systems. The concept has been a missing link, overlooked in part because most analyses have been overly concentrated on the seemingly "large" aspects— the general state structure, the periodic state plan, the growth of bureaucratic machinery—and have not searched for the "small" forms that persist at the levels where academic work takes place. The general understanding of academic organization to date has also been biased by a heavy concentration of research on the American system, which, in worldwide perspective, is a deviant case of national academic structure, not least in the way that guild control has been muted. Attention to the underlying structure of academic action has also been undermined by fascination with such dramatic aspects of systems as the student protest of the late 1960s and such immediate problems as rapid development of staff and facilities during periods of student expansion and painful contraction during times of enrollment decline and decreased funding.

In this study we have observed an Italian variant of a European mode, since throughout the Continent the general structure of academic organization combines faculty guild and state bureaucracy. Each of these major forms has had a long history. Along with the origination of the guild clusters in the late medieval period came the beginnings of a superstructure of public supervision, as city-states and other temporal authorities attempted to regulate the academic bodies. But the bureaucratic forms developed genuine strength only later, as state authority in one country after another became more inclusive and applied modern means of administration. Nation-building in Western Europe meant the encapsulation of higher education in one or more public bureaus. The full nationalization of higher education, in which all or nearly all units were placed under one or more ministries of the national government, was modeled to the world by France, especially after Napoleon. The federal variant of public control developed in Germany, where universities became increasingly a part of an educational bureau of the *Länder* governments. In either the national or federal variant, the primary structure of control came to express two sets of interests. The interests of senior academics were strongly fixed in the chair, its related roles, and the collegial bodies that ruled the faculty and the university; those of public officials were rooted in the central and field offices of the education ministry. And the organization of the interests of the professors had historical primacy; emerging governmental frameworks of new nations had to embrace existing faculties and universities that had retained guild properties.

In cross-national perspective, the European mode is noteworthy for concentration of power at the bottom and the top of the levels of organization found within provincial and national systems. The middle levels of faculty and university are controlled from below, by chair-dominance of local rule, and from above, by bureaucratic tools of central administration and the devices elaborated by the chairs for national rule. One does not find independent sources of power in the middle: there is little between professors and the state officials. The weakness of university-wide administration helps explain the paradox that extensive nationalization of higher education, as in France and Italy, can go hand in hand with autonomy in the comparatively unsupervised chairs, institutes, and faculties. There is no administrative class in sites close to actual operations. This has led to a weakness in attention to problems of the university as an entity, since those who do have local power have primary interests in the parts. The top-bottom pattern of state bureaucracy and faculty guild, missing a strong middle, has generally reduced corporate cohesiveness and identity at the level of the university.

At the same time, this common Continental combination of faculty guild and public ministry reduces competition among institutions and hence the play of market forces. The guild clusters concentrate on monopolizing their own local domains of work; the governmental bureau concentrates on system-wide uniform administration. With the combined controls of guild and bureaucracy predominating over the indirect order (or disorder) of competitive market forces, academics increase their personal effectiveness by maneuvering within the control system instead of maneuvering within the market. Thus in the French and other nationalized systems, as well as in Italy, academics have been impelled to extend the guild devices that serve their interests from local to national domains. This tendency is lessened in the German system, since academics there are not all bound together within a single national formal domain of activity but can maneuver somewhat among the separate *Land* systems of academic control. But there also remains little doubt that, within the *Land* systems, the German professors have used the guild pattern of autocracy-within-collegiality to a high degree.

There is also little doubt that the British mode of academic organization has been rooted in a substructure of academic guilds but with important differences from the combination of interests vested in the European mode. The state bureaucracy has had a lesser hand. As chartered corporations composed of chartered colleges that developed their own endowment, Oxford and Cambridge developed extensive autonomy from the controls of local and national departments of government. Distinctively different regional subsystems developed in Scotland and Wales; the University of London became a unique academic holding company for the nation and the empire, with branch colleges not only in England but also in India, Ceylon, Africa, and the West Indies; and the nineteenth-century civic universities leaned in their evolution more toward the autonomous model of Oxford and Cambridge than the state-coordinated universities of the Continent.

In the British pattern of remote state supervision, collegial control has flourished, particularly in the two institutions, Oxford and Cambridge, whose historical primacy and towering prestige have subtly defined the British style of academic control. Immensely elaborate patterns of collegial control have developed in the operating web of chairs, departments, faculties, colleges, and universities, at a price, of course, of often slowing decision-making to a crawl or paralyzing it completely. But the guild patterns have not operated alone at the institutional level, especially outside of Oxford and Cambridge, since laymen have been systematically included in some of the governing bodies and a key administrative position has been provided in the vice-chancellorship. Analyses of the British university agree that the vice-chancellor is typically an important force in the politics and administration of the campus.[33] His independent responsibility, and that of some laymen, for the welfare of the whole, has apparently helped tilt guild interests toward a similar responsibility. In any event, compared to those on the Continent, institutions have been considerably responsible for their own administration: from that situation has flowed corporate pride and identity. Guild authority has had an important role and continues to do so, but it generally has not achieved a local monopoly of academic power. Instead of the top-bottom pattern of faculty guild and state bureaucracy found on the Continent, there is a strengthened middle and weaker top in Britain. The test is that the faculty clusters must relate primarily to administrators and laymen who hold university-level responsibilities rather than to officials in a central government bureau. Bureaucratic and trustee principles of authority have been intimately interfused with the collegial and autocratic rights inherent in the guild principles of authority.

But the British intermixture is but a half-way house to the extensive fusion of guild organization with a plurality of other forms of authority that is found in the United States. In the historical development of the American system, trustee control came first in time, as small independent colleges were established by religious interests, at first slowly in the colonial period and then multiplying rapidly in the westward expansion of the nineteenth century. Organization at the local level was from the top down, with a board of laymen made responsible for the enterprise and free to hire and fire teachers and a president. There was no guild organization on the part of either faculty or students, as on the Continent or in Britain; instead, the original building block was the unitary college. Then, as private and public *universities* developed in the nineteenth century, the device of a board of trustees was carried into their management. It became the chief American mechanism for reconciling public accountability and the professional autonomy of academicians and their institutions, in sharp contrast to the assumption on the Continent and in most countries of the world that a governmental ministry was the appropriate mechanism.

It was within the framework of this mechanism that bureaucrats and professors had to find their way to power. Bureaucratic administration developed primarily within the institution itself, rather than within a higher state ministry. Since the trustees, and not a state minister, were formally responsible, administrative services became grouped under the trustees in the form of campus administration, rather than developing at some level above the campus. As a result, by the turn of the twentieth century strong campus bureaucracy had become a second distinctive form in the American mode of governance.[34] And last in the evolutionary chain came the development of tools of faculty influence. As they emerged, they were conditioned by the existence of administrative as well as trustee authority and had to be blended with both *within* the unitary nature of organization that had been established.

When, in the nineteenth century, the American college and university required subdivisions in order to group specialties, they developed the department as an operating unit. The department became both a collegial order and bureaucratic arm.[35] Within it, personal rule could obtain in the specialties of senior professors and the faculty members could together decide on certain matters, much in the style of chairholding professors on the Continent. An ideological claim to guild rule was elaborated—a claim that recalled the oldest traditions of the university, that pointed to the nineteenth-century German model of the research university, and that centered on the concept of freedom of teaching and research. But the department was also the lowest unit in an administrative structure: the chairman was responsible to administrative superiors as well as to colleagues, so much so that he became a classic and enduring case of the managerial man-in-the-middle—the person caught between "management" and "the workers." Professors have had to win their way to collegial primacy in matters of curriculum and selection of personnel within the context of established powers of a strong local administration.

In the twentieth century the extent to which professors have achieved power has varied widely among the diverse sectors of American higher education. Generally faculty influence is greater in institutions high in prestige, older in age, private in ownership, and furthest from the influence of school administration. Faculty influence has been relatively low in the public community college, with its origins in American secondary-school organization, and in the state college, which evolved from a primary mission of teacher training. The relatively weak power position of teachers in these settings has been exacerbated by the rapid growth in scale and complexity of these organizations in the years since World War II and particularly by the addition and growth of higher levels of administration over them in state systems. As a result of increasing bureaucratic dominance and the weakness of guild forms, instructors have been strongly inclined to join faculty unions as a new form of faculty influence. But the union mechanism adds yet another set of officials, those of the union, to the mix of groups whose interests become vested in legitimate rights. And although craft unions retain some guildlike properties in their internal operations, large modern unions tend to be bureaucratic and oligarchical. In their development in the American academic world, they apparently still reduce rather than enhance the combination of personal and collegial rule that is the essence of guild authority. In cross-national comparison, the American structure is studded with power groups at the middle level of campus and multicampus organization.

Thus, the guild authority of local clusters of faculty is variously combined with other types of authority in the European mode, the British mode, and the American mode of academic organization—and, we may expect, in other modes found around the world. The blends of authority are so subtle and complex that the guild form is often difficult to perceive. In this regard, comparative and historical perspectives help greatly; study of the history of the Italian system, where the guild form is strongly expressed, and of other systems on the Continent, makes clear that the original form of university organization was never put to flight but has endured through the centuries.

Much remains to be explained about the considerable persistence of personal and collegial rule in academic organization. The capacity appears rooted in necessity as well as in vested interest—in the fact that universities and colleges must compose themselves around a set of disciplines to a degree not found in any other modern organizations. Since the disciplines are carriers of advanced knowledge, the answer to the question of why guild authority persists apparently involves the relationship of social organization to esoteric knowledge. It does appear that academics trade in skills that cannot develop under too severe constraints of bureaucratic and political dictate. On this crucial matter, the world is now alive with totalitarian, authoritarian, and democratic experiments in strong state control. The blends of academic and state authority that develop in different countries and regions of the world will determine much about the future viability of their systems of higher education.

It may be that political authorities, planners, and bureaucrats, like irresistible forces, will roll over and submerge traditional forms of faculty influence. But both the eight centuries of university history since the beginning in Bologna and the growing strength of professional organization suggest that this will not occur. Instead, the future is likely to find a medieval institution, the guild, still exhibiting a capacity to bend according to the times and thereby to persist as a crucial part of academic structure.

NOTES

CHAPTER ONE

1. Hastings Rashdall, *The Universities of Europe in the Middle Ages*, 1:97.

2. Ibid.; Charles Homer Haskins, *The Rise of Universities*, p. 7; P. J. Jones, "Communes and Despots," *Transactions of the Royal Historical Society*, 15:79–80.

3. Rashdall, *Universities of Europe*, 1:148–51; Haskins, *Rise of Universities*, pp. 9–10; John W. Baldwin and Richard A. Goldthwaite, eds., *Universities in Politics*, pp. 5–6, 40–46; Alan B. Cobban, "Medieval Student Power," *Past and Present*, no. 53, pp. 38–40, 44–45, 61–64.

4. Rashdall, *Universities of Europe*, 1:151.

5. R. Freeman Butts, *The Education of the West*, pp. 171–77; Haskins, *Rise of Universities*, pp. 4–5.

6. Daniel Waley, *The Italian City-Republics*, p. 101.

7. Rashdall, *Universities of Europe*, 2:2–21.

8. Ibid., 1:221–24.

9. Ibid., 2:22, 28.

10. Ibid., 1:165.

11. Ibid., 1:218; 2:61–62.

12. Cobban, "Medieval Student Power," pp. 44–48; Butts, *Education of the West*, p. 179.

13. Cobban, "Medieval Student Power," pp. 36–37, 42–48; Christopher Driver, *The Exploding University*, pp. 85–87.

14. Jones, "Communes and Despots," pp. 74–78, 83–85.

15. Ibid., p. 85.

16. Rashdall, *Universities of Europe*, 1:152–53. See also Sylvia L. Thrupp, "The Gilds," in *Economic Organization and Policies in the Middle Ages*, ed. M. M. Postan, E. E. Rich, and Edward Miller, pp. 230–80.

17. Jones, "Communes and Despots," p. 95.

18. Butts, *Education of the West*, pp. 158–59; quoted from and based on Rushton Coulborn, ed., *Feudalism in History*, pp. 4–5.

19. Cobban, "Medieval Student Power," p. 58, 58n.

20. Rashdall, *Universities of Europe*, 2:59–60.

21. Richard Hofstadter and Walter P. Metzger, *The Development of Academic Freedom in the United States*. See especially chap. 1, "The European Heritage," and chap. 3, "The Colonial Colleges."

22. Rashdall, *Universities of Europe*, 2:59–62. See also Nathan Schachner, *The Medieval Universities*, chap. 28, "The Italian Universities." Schachner concluded that the early Italian universities had "almost complete independence of ecclesiastical control" (p. 287). See also Hofstadter and Metzger, *Academic Freedom*, chap. 1, "The European Heritage," who, noting that "a separate faculty of theology had no place in the early organization of the Italian unversities . . . and in later stages of the universities' development the study of theology was given but secondary or slight importance," have concluded that "the Italian universities were somewhat secular in their preoccupations" and that "ecclesiastical interference was comparatively moderate, and, when exercised, was the instrument of political rather than doctrinal objectives" (p. 4).

23. Denys Hay, "Schools and Universities," in *The New Cambridge Modern History*, 2:418, 433.

24. Eric Cochrane, *Florence in the Forgotten Centuries*, pp. 59–62.

25. As put by Richard L. Kagan, "The universities of early modern Europe are unfortunate in that they have never merited a study comparable to H. Rashdall, *The Universities of Europe in the Middle Ages*." Although a few works of a general nature are available on England and Germany, nothing on a broad scale has existed either for Italy or France. Richard L. Kagan, *Students and Society in Early Modern Spain*, p. 269; see "Bibliographical Essay," pp. 262–71.

26. Matthew Arnold, *Schools and Universities on the Continent*, p. 111.

27. Personal communication from Richard L. Kagan, drawing on his unpublished data for these countries, and, on Spain, from his *Students and Society*; also, Arnold, *Schools and Universities*, chap. 11, "The Italian Universities."

28. Joseph Ben-David, *The Scientist's Role in Society*, pp. 50–55.

29. Ibid., p. 59.

30. Ibid., pp. 59–66.

31. Ibid., p. 67.

32. Thrupp, "The Gilds," p. 280.

33. See Marjorie Reeves, "The European University from Medieval Times," in *Higher Education: Demand & Response*, ed. W. R. Niblett, pp. 61–84.

34. Carlo M. Cipolla, "The Economic Decline of Italy," in *Crisis and Change in the Venetian Economy*, ed., Brian S. Pullan, pp. 127-45.

35. Denys Hay, "Introduction," in *The New Cambridge Modern History*, 1:7.

36. Butts, *Education of the West*, p. 223.

37. The universities are Turin, Milan, Pavia, Padua, Bologna, Florence, Pisa, Rome, and Naples. Comitato di studio dei problemi dell'Università italiana, *La popolazione universitaria*, 1:136-37.

38. Edith E. Coulson James, *Bologna*, pp. 159-60; Arnold, *Schools and Universities*, pp. 109-10. The *claimed* figures for the early period run as high as 10,000 to 20,000.

39. Arnold, *Schools and Universities*, p. 113.

40. Frederick Harbison and Charles A. Myers, *Education, Manpower and Economic Growth*, pp. 31-34.

41. There were many lower nonteaching staff, especially in faculties of medicine, to provide physical plant services and to handle a growing amount of bureaucratic paperwork. Estimates at the end of the 1960s placed their number as equal to that of all teaching personnel. Sergio Bruno, "Dimensioni economiche di una riforma universitaria," p. 143.

42. Organisation for Economic Co-operation and Development (OECD), *Development of Higher Education, 1950-1967. Analytical Report*, Table II-5, p. 81.

43. OECD, *Development of Higher Education, 1950-1967. Statistical Survey*, p. 437.

44. OECD, *Italy*, p. 20.

45. OECD, *Higher Education. Analytical Report*, p. 163.

46. Centro studi investimenti sociali (CENSIS), "Scuola, famiglia e mobilità sociale," pp. 20-28.

47. Comparison made by CENSIS, an Italian research organization, using a method devised by the American economist T. W. Schultz. CENSIS, "I livelli medi di istruzione della popolazione in Italia e negli Stati Uniti," pp. 13-15.

48. OECD, *Italy*, p. 20.

49. Ibid.

50. Italy, Istituto centrale di statistica, *Annuario statistico dell'istruzione italiana*, 19 (1967): p. xiii.

51. OECD, *Higher Education. Analytical Report*, p. 40. Among the best-known of the nonuniversity institutions have been institutes in Venice for architecture, economics and commerce, and foreign languages and literature.

52. Ibid., pp. 40-41.

53. Luciano Cappelletti, "The Italian Bureaucracy," p. 92.

54. Data supplied by Giampaolo Bonani in unpublished paper, Rome Conference on Italian Higher Education, International Council for Educational Development, July 1972.

55. A new university opened in Calabria in the fall of 1972 and small places began to develop under local initiatives in the late 1960s and early 1970s. See chap. 4.

56. Italy, Istituto centrale di statistica, *Annuario statistico*, 14 (1962).

57. James, *Bologna*, p. 173.

CHAPTER TWO

1. See epigraph at beginning of this chapter.

2. Robert C. Fried, *The Italian Prefects*, chaps. 1, 2. On the preconditions and early history of the new nation, see also: Denis Mack Smith, *Italy*, sections 1–4; Christopher Seton-Watson, *Italy From Liberalism to Fascism, 1870–1925*, prologue and chap. 1; John A. Thayer, *Italy and the Great War*, chaps. 1–3; Guido de Ruggiero, *The History of European Liberalism*, chap. 4, "Italian Liberalism."

3. Fried, *Italian Prefects*, p. 57.

4. Ibid., pp. 17–20.

5. The Kingdom of the Two Sicilies (Sicily and the southern half of the peninsular mainland); the Papal States in the center of the peninsula; the Kingdom of Lombardy-Venetia, part of the Austrian Empire; the Duchies of Tuscany, Parma, Modena, and Lucca, under Austrian princes; and Piedmont. Fried, *Italian Prefects*, p. 51.

6. Ibid., pp. 55–56.

7. Ibid., pp. 34–51.

8. Ibid., p. 36.

9. Ibid., pp. 48–49.

10. R. C. Simonini, Jr., *The Universities of Italy*, pp. 4–5.

11. Dante Germino and Stefano Passigli, *The Government and Politics of Contemporary Italy*, pp. 145, 143.

12. Universal manhood suffrage came as late as the period between 1912 and 1919. Germino and Passigli, *Contemporary Italy*, pp. 4, 30; Fried, *Italian Prefects*, p. 158.

13. Fried, *Italian Prefects*, p. 298.

14. Ibid., p. 139.

15. Marzio Barbagli, *Disoccupazione intellettuale e sistema scolastico in Italia*, pp. 65–68.

16. Fried, *Italian Prefects*, p. 174.

17. Ibid., p. 193.

18. Ibid., p. 176.

19. Germino and Passigli, *Contemporary Italy*, pp. 75–77; Fried, *Italian Prefects*, p. 222.

20. Luciano Cappelletti, "The Italian Bureaucracy," p. 3.

21. Fried, *Italian Prefects*, p. 141.

22. Harold Seidman, *Politics, Position & Power*, p. 162.

23. Ibid., p. 138.

24. Ernesto Rossi, quoted in John Clarke Adams and Paolo Barile, *The Government of Republican Italy*, p. 221.

25. Germino and Passigli, *Contemporary Italy*, p. 163.

26. Joseph La Palombara, *Interest Groups in Italian Politics*, chap. 8.

27. Ibid., p. 262.

28. Ibid., chap. 9.

29. Ibid., p. 372.

30. Adams and Barile, *Republican Italy*, chap. 9, "The Judicial System"; Mauro Cappelletti, John Henry Merryman, and Joseph M. Perillo, *The Italian Legal System*, chaps. 5–7; Norberto Bobbio, "Trends in Italian Legal Theory," pp. 329–40; Giorgio Freddi, "Legitimacy and Opposition in the Italian Judiciary," pp. 64–75.

31. La Palombara, *Interest Groups*, p. 372.

32. Ibid., p. 373.

33. Ibid., p. 391.

34. On interpretation in Italian law, within a system where application is supposed to be heavily prefigured by the dictates of established doctrine and legislative law, see Cappelletti, Merryman, and Perillo, *Italian Legal System*, chap. 7, "The Italian Style: Interpretation."

35. Robert O. Berdahl, *British Universities and the State*; Graeme C. Moodie and Rowland Eustace, *Power and Authority in British Universities*.

36. John H. Van de Graaff, "Germany," in *Academic Power*, ed. John H. Van de Graaff.

37. Matthew Arnold, *Schools and Universities on the Continent*, pp. 118–19, 136.

38. Sergio Bruno, "Dimensioni economiche di una riforma universitaria," p. 145.

39. A general description of Italian university finance may be found in Comitato di studio dei problemi dell'Università italiana, *Finanziamento e spese dell'Università*, pp. 3–94.

40. On sunk costs and budgetary rigidity in large organizations generally, and particularly in the public sector, see Herbert Kaufman, *The Limits of Organizational Change*, pp. 23–31; Hugh Heclo and Aaron Wildavsky, *The Private Government of Public Money*, pp. 21–29, 169–81.

41. This system was altered in 1969–70; see chap. 4 on attempted reforms of the nationalized curriculum.

42. Italy, Ministero della pubblica istruzione, *Disposizioni sull'ordinamento didattico universitario*.

43. Italy, Ministero della pubblica istruzione, *Università e istituti universitari*.

44. Alberto Caracciolo, "Autonomia o centralizzazione degli studi superiori nella età della destra," pp. 573–603; Barbagli, *Disoccupazione intellettuale*, pp. 70–80.

45. Simonini, *Universities of Italy*, pp. 4–5.

46. Ibid., p. 5; Barbagli, *Disoccupazione intellettuale*, pp. 197–98.

47. Simonini, *Universities of Italy*, p. 5.

48. Some 25 to 30 percent of all students were in the *fuori corso* status in the years around 1960. Sergio Bruno, "Dimensioni economiche," table 1, p. 124; see also "Rapporto tra studenti iscritti in corso e professori (ordinari, straordinari e incaricati)," and "Rapporto tra popolazione studentesca totale e professori (ordinari, straordinari e incaricati)," ibid., table 7, p. 126.

49. See Burton R. Clark, "The 'Cooling-Out' Function in Higher Education," pp. 569–76; idem, *The Open Door College*, chap. 5.

50. As expansion in enrollment outdistanced expansion in chairs *and* as the chairholders sometimes found other things to do, the second level of teaching personnel—*professori incaricati*—were increasingly assigned basic courses, doing work similar to that of the full professors. See chaps. 3, 4.

51. As in other countries, the certification of competence by the formal education system itself is backstopped in some occupations by further examination that may be somewhat more universal in quality (for example, the bar examination for lawyers in the United States). National state examinations (*esami di stato*), or profession-administered examinations, qualify university graduates for professional practice in such fields as law, medicine, engineering, and architecture. There are also state-administered competitions for entrance into secondary-school teaching. But these latter examinations have not affected the discretion of the individual professor in determining who achieves university graduation. The results of the national state examinations in medicine and some seven other profesional fields are reported in annual educational statistics: See Italy, Istituto centrale di statistica, *Annuario statistico dell'istruzione italiana*, vol. 24, p. 310. For a description of nationwide competitive examinations operated by a profession, in this case for the selection of judges, see Giorgio Freddi, "Legitimacy and Opposition in the Italian Judiciary," pp. 36–41.

52. The legally established rules of the system have been compiled in Giuseppe Jorio, *Legislazione universitaria*. They are also found in a two-volume, 6,000-page compilation of Italian administrative law: Aldo M. Sandulli, *Codice della legislazione amministrativa*.

53. Jorio, *Legislazione*, pp. 268–70, "Assistenti Volontari." Some forty-five pages of this volume of rules were devoted to the category of assistants.

54. Guido Martinotti, "Italy," in *Students, University and Society*,

ed. Margaret Scotford Archer, p. 182. Basic data on categories of assistants and the nature of their activities are available in: Italy, Istituto di statistica, Facoltà di scienze statistiche demografiche ed attuariali, Università degli studi di Roma, *Gli assistenti universitari e i liberi docenti in Italia.*

55. Jorio, *Legislazione*, p. 231.

56. Ibid., pp. 234-35.

57. Ibid., sections on "Concorsi" and "Commissioni giudicatrici," pp. 141-46, within the section on "Professori di ruolo," pp. 133-74; and Sandulli, *Codice*, pp. 1804-7.

58. On selection of professors in Germany, see John H. Van de Graaff, "The Politics of German University Reform, 1810-1970," pp. 106-11.

59. On "exit" versus "voice" as a means of influence of members in various kinds of social systems, see Albert O. Hirschman, *Exit, Voice, and Loyalty.*

60. Italy, *Ruoli di anzianità del personale insegnante delle università e degli istituti superiori d'istruzione* [Seniority Lists of the Teaching Personnel of the Universities and the Institutes of Higher Education].

61. Ibid., p. 53.

62. Regolamento Generale Universitario, approvato con R.D. (Regio decreto) 6 aprile 1924, n. 674; Testo Unico delle leggi sull'Istruzione Superiore, approvato con R.D. 31 agosto 1933, n. 1592; and Regolamento sugli studenti, i titoli accademici gli esami di Stato e l'assistenza scolastica nelle Università e negli Istituti Superiori, approvato con R.D. 4 giugno 1938, n. 1269.

63. Indice delle circolari in ordine cronologico and Disposizioni legislative e regolamentari in ordine cronologico, in Jorio, *Legislazione*, pp. 1015-35.

64. Ibid., p. 166.

65. Ibid., passim.

66. See, in the general organizational literature, Melville Dalton, *Men Who Manage*, chaps. 9, 10; Andrew Frank, "Goal Ambiguity and Conflicting Standards," pp. 8-13; and Charles E. Lindblom, "The Science of 'Muddling Through'," pp. 79-88.

67. Jorio, *Legislazione*, p. 13.

68. Ibid., p. 19.

69. Ibid., pp. 16-19, 21-24.

70. Fried, *Italian Prefects*, p. 274.

71. See Herbert Kaufman, *The Forest Ranger*, pp. 25-87.

72. Ibid., pp. 91-200.

73. On four types of interorganizational relations (unitary, federative, coalitional, and social choice), see Roland L. Warren, "The Interorganizational Field as a Focus for Investigation," pp. 396-419.

CHAPTER THREE

1. Harold Seidman, *Politics, Position, & Power*, pp. 31-36.

2. Grant McConnell, *Private Power and American Democracy*, p. 7.

3. See Robert C. Fried, *The Italian Prefects*; Joseph La Palombara, *Interest Groups in Italian Politics.*

4. La Palombara, *Interest Groups*, p. 391.

5. Organisation for Economic Co-operation and Development (OECD), *Reviews of National Science Policies: Italy* ("The Brooks Report"), pp. 88-89, 195-96.

6. Data from national survey reported in Pier Paolo Giglioli, "The Italian University between Patrimonialism and Bureaucracy."

7. Martinotti has argued that there is a strong psychology of scarcity at work in the division of the resources that come down the main administrative line, one that pressures professors to seek resources through additional means. Guido Martinotti, "Italy," in *Students, University & Society*, ed. Margaret Scotford Archer, pp. 188-89.

8. OECD, *Science Policies: Italy*, p. 92.

9. Italy, Istituto di statistica, Facoltà di scienze statistiche demografiche ed attuariali, Università degli studi di Roma, *Gli assistenti universitari e i liberi docenti in Italia*, pp. 106-15.

10. Martinotti, "Italy," p. 194, n. 15.

11. Italy, Istituto di statistica, Facoltà di scienze statistiche demografiche ed attuariali, Università degli studi di Roma, *Gli assistenti*, pp. 108-9.

12. As, for example, in Martinotti, "Italy," pp. 171-72.

13. Gordon J. Di Renzo, "Sociology in Italy Today," pp. 1-26.

14. Comitato di studio dei problemi dell'Università italiana, *La popolazione universitaria*, 1:136-49; see also Martinotti, "Italy," pp. 183-87.

15. On the general distribution of authority in the German university system, see the chapter on the Federal Republic of Germany in John H. Van de Graaff, ed., *Academic Power.*

16. Terry Nichols Clark, *Prophets and Patrons*, chap. 2. See also Robert Gilpin, *France in the Age of the Scientific State*, chap. 4, "The Heritage of the Napoleonic System"; the chapter on academic control in France in Van de Graaff, ed., *Academic Power*; and Michelle Patterson, "Conflict, Power, and Structure."

17. William J. Goode, "A Theory of Role Strain," pp. 483-96; Robert K. Merton, *Social Theory and Social Structure*, chap. 9, "Continuities in the Theory of Reference Groups and Social Structure"; J. Diedrick Snoek, "Role Strain in Diversified Role Sets," pp. 363-72.

18. For a general statement of these four rewards of role accumulation, see Sam D. Seiber, "Toward a Theory of Role Accumulation," pp. 567-78.

19. Giuseppe Jorio, *Legislazione universitaria*, pp. 19-24.

20. Comitato di studio dei problemi dell'Università italiana, *Finanziamento e spese dell'Università*, pp. 8-11.

21. Comitato di studio dei problemi dell'Università italiana, *La popolazione universitaria*, pp. 151-54. This study reported that in thirteen out of twenty-one universities examined, one or more of the agents designated by local institutions were chairholders; thus outside organs have "the tendency to renounce their even limited power of control" (p. 153).

22. A parallel finding on Italian politicians has been noted by Robert D. Putnam: the more "ideological" politicians, especially on the Left, are not afraid to compromise. They are as much open to the bargaining of pluralist politics as their nonideological peers. Putnam, *The Beliefs of Politicians*, pp. 52-56, 61-62.

23. Robert Michels, *Political Parties*.

24. Ibid., passim; Franco Ferrarotti, "Management in Italy," in *Management in the Industrial World*, ed. F. Harbison and C. A. Myers, pp. 239-40; Arnold S. Tannenbaum et al., *Hierarchy in Organizations*, pp. 43, 123; Norman Kogan, *The Government of Italy*, pp. 64-65.

25. Comitato di studio dei problemi dell'Università italiana, *La popolazione universitaria*, pp. 153-54.

26. Aldo M. Sandulli, *Codice della legislazione amministrativa*, 1:1804-7.

27. Jorio, *Legislazione*, p. 824: Ministerial decree, September 15, 1966, naming the persons who would serve for the four-year period, 1966-70.

28. OECD, *Science Policies: Italy*, pp. 45-47; and Italy, Consiglio nazionale delle ricerche, *Relazione del Presidente del C.N.R. sullo stato della ricerca scientifica e technologica in Italia per il 1973*.

29. Comitato di studio dei problemi dell'Università italiana, *La popolazione universitaria*, p. 154; Jorio, *Legislazione*, p. 863.

30. OECD, *Science Policies: Italy*, pp. 46-47.

31. Ibid., p. 60.

32. Ibid., p. 45.

33. Sandulli, *Codice*, p. 1806.

34. Ibid., p. 1807.

35. Ibid., p. 1805.

36. Felice Froio, *Università: Mafia e Potere*, chap. 11, "La mafia delle cattedre," pp. 169-76.

37. Ibid., p. 173.

38. Ibid., pp. 171-72.

39. Ibid., pp. 175-76.

40. This power is held also by bureau professionals in many balkanized sectors of modern American government. Seidman, *Politics*, p. 275.

41. John Clarke Adams and Paolo Barile, *The Government of Repub-*

lican Italy, pp. 63–66; La Palombara, *Interest Groups*, pp. 109–10; Giorgio Galli and Alfonso Prandi, *Patterns of Political Participation in Italy*, pp. 271–74.

42. Galli and Prandi, *Political Participation*, pp. 271–74.

43. Adams and Barile, *Republican Italy*, p. 65.

44. *I Deputati e Senatori del Quinto Parlamento Repubblicano*, pp. 455 and 728 for committee membership, and passim for biographical occupational information.

45. Woodrow Wilson, *Congressional Government*, p. 76.

46. McConnell, *Private Power*, p. 352, and especially Seidman, *Politics,* chap. 2.

47. Guido de Ruggiero, *The History of European Liberalism*, p. viii.

48. Fried, *Italian Prefects*, p. 217.

49. H. Stuart Hughes, *Consciousness and Society*, p. 201.

50. Denis Mack Smith, *Italy*, p. 252. See also Cecil Sprigge, *Benedetto Croce*.

51. Even the giants of the early leadership of the Italian Communist party, Gramsci and Togliatti, were followers of Crocean thought, and excellent students of the humanities, before converting to Marxism. Dante Germino and Stefano Passigli, *The Government and Politics of Contemporary Italy*, p. 180.

52. Hughes, *Consciousness*, p. 208.

53. Comitato di studio dei problemi dell'Università italiana, *La popolazione universitaria*, pp. 130–33. This study speaks of "the strong influence that the German culture exercised on the atmosphere of the Italian university" (p. 133).

54. See Felice Froio, *Università e classe politica*, especially chap. 2.

55. "Personal rulership ... is an ineradicable component of the public and private bureaucracies of highly industrialized countries," as well as often being the dominant form of government in the new states of the twentieth century. "Far from being a vanishing phenomenon, personal rulership in public bureaucracies is apparently enlarged by the extension of government functions in industrialized countries." Guenther Roth, "Personal Rulership, Patrimonialism, and Empire-Building in the New States," pp. 196, 199.

56. Under patrimonialism, "the position of authority as such is still traditionally legitimized, but not the detailed structure of carrying it out which is, on the contrary, a 'right' of the chief to do what he will within his sphere of personal prerogative." Talcott Parsons, Introduction, in *Max Weber: The Theory of Social and Economic Organization*, p. 63. On the application of this Weberian concept to the Italian academic profession, see Pier Paolo Giglioli, *L'Università italiana tra patrimonialismo e burocrazia*, available in English as "The Italian University between Patrimonialism and Bureaucracy."

57. See A. M. Carr-Saunders and P. A. Wilson, *The Professions*; Talcott Parsons, "Professions," in *International Encyclopedia of the Social Sciences*, 12: 536-47; William J. Goode, "The Theoretical Limits of Professionalization," in Amitai Etzioni, *The Semi-Professions and Their Organization*, pp. 266-313.

58. Walter Metzger, "The Academic Profession and Its Public Critics," in *The Public Challenge and the Campus Response*, ed., Robert A. Altman and Carolyn M. Byerly, p. 73.

59. Ibid., p. 73.

60. Ibid., pp. 81-82.

61. See Eliot Freidson, *Professional Dominance*, Chap. 5, "Professional Dominance and the Ordering of Health Services"; H. Jamous and B. Peloille, "Changes in the French University-Hospital System," in *Professions and Professionalization*, ed. J. A. Jackson, pp. 111-52.

62. Freidson, *Professional Dominance*, pp. 151-61.

63. Terry Clark, *Prophets*, chap. 2; Gilpin, *France*, chap. 4; Patterson, "Conflict," chaps. 3, 4.

64. See Diana Crane, *Invisible Colleges*.

65. See Harry G. Johnson, "National Styles in Economic Research," pp. 65-74.

66. OECD, *Science Policies: Italy*; Johnson, "National Styles."

CHAPTER FOUR

1. Eric Ashby, "The Structure of Higher Education," p. 7.

2. F. Roy Willis, *Italy Chooses Europe*, p. 72; see also chaps. 4, 5. On the development of Italian industry and economy, see also: Vera Lutz, *Italy*; George Hildebrand, *Growth and Structure in the Economy of Modern Italy*; Joe S. Bain, *International Differences in Industrial Structure*.

3. Organisation for Economic Co-operation and Development (OECD), *Reviews of National Science Policies: Italy* ("The Brooks Report"), pp. 93-94.

4. Italy, Istituto centrale di statistica, *Annuario statistico dell'istruzione*.

5. Ashby, "Structure of Higher Education," p. 7.

6. See Felice Froio, *Università e classe politica*. Some changes made in 1969 and the early 1970s are discussed later in the chapter.

7. The third of Ashby's "three main environmental forces"; see his "Structure of Higher Education," p. 7.

8. Italy, Istituto centrale di statistica, *Annuario statistico*, volumes reporting the respective years.

9. Ibid.

10. OECD, *Quantitative Trends in Teaching Staff in Higher Education*, pp. 121-27.

11. OECD, *Science Policies: Italy*. Highly critical articles on the "Research Climate in Italy" also appeared in the American journal *Science* in 1964 and 1965 (vol. 145, August 14, 1964, pp. 690–93; vol. 148, April 9, 1965, pp. 205–7).

12. For example, Adriano Buzzati-Traverso et al., *L'organizzazione della ricerca scientifica*; Emilio Sanna, "I cervelli en esilio," *Tempo* 31 (March 8, 1969):20–26; and the column entitled "Scienza e Società," in *L'Espresso* during 1969.

13. For the best account of the rise and fall of the Italian student movement, along with such movements elsewhere in Europe, see Gianni Statera, *Death of a Utopia*, especially chaps. 3, 5. See also Federico Mancini, "The Italian Student Movement," pp. 427–32; idem, "From Reform to Adventure," pp. 413–22; and Guido Martinotti, "Italy," in *Students, University and Society*, ed. Margaret Scotford Archer, pp. 189–93.

14. See especially Statera, *Utopia*, chap. 5.

15. Ibid., pp. 69–70. The UNURI (the National Union of Italian Student Representative Bodies) was actually a loosely joined association of many student associations organized along lines of affiliation with Italian political parties and major factions within them: for example, associations of left-wing Catholics or of Socialist and Communist students.

16. On the nature of the general problem, see Jeffrey L. Pressman and Aaron B. Wildavsky, *Implementation*.

17. Froio, *Università e classe politica*, chap. 2.

18. Ibid., chap. 3; Italy, Ministero della pubblica istruzione, *Relazione della commissione di indagine sullo stato e sullo sviluppo della pubblica istruzione in Italia* and *Relazione sullo stato della pubblica istruzione in Italia*.

19. Froio, *Università e classe politica*, chap. 4.

20. Pier Paolo Giglioli, "The Italian University between Patrimonialism and Bureaucracy."

21. Statera, *Utopia*, p. 258.

22. Legge 30 novembre, n. 766 (Conversione in legge, con modificazioni, del decreto-legge 1 ottobre 1973, n. 580, recante misure urgenti per l'università). *Gazzetta Ufficiale della Repubblica Italiana*. Parte Prima. Rome: Sabato, 1 Dicembre 1973.

23. Legge n. 766, "Art. 1. (Nuovi posti di professore universitario di ruolo)."

24. Legge n. 766, "Art. 2. (Nuovi norme per i concorsi a posti di professore universitario)."

25. Legge n. 766, "Art. 3. (Inquadramento nei ruoli del personale docente universitario)."

26. Legge n. 766, "Art. 4. (Stabilizzazione dei professori e nuova disciplina del conferimento degli incarichi)."

27. Legge n. 766, "Art. 9. (Nuova norme sugli organi universitari)."

28. Legge n. 766, "Art. 10. (Nuove università)."

29. Statera, *Utopia*, pp. 97–100; Italy, Istituto centrale di statistica, *Annuario statistico*, 1972, pp. 320–21.

30. Italy, Istituto centrale di statistica, *Annuario statistico*, 1972, pp. 275, 320–21.

31. Ibid.

32. Harold Seidman, *Politics, Position, & Power*, p. 27.

33. Charles E. Lindblom, "The Science of 'Muddling Through'," pp. 79–88.

34. Charles E. Lindblom, *The Intelligence of Democracy.*

35. See Philip Selznick, "The Sociology of Law," in *International Encyclopedia of the Social Sciences*, 9:56.

36. See James L. Sundquist, *Dispersing Population*, Chap. 4, "Italy: Two Societies, Two Economies," especially pp. 166–68. An extensive assessment of planning practices in Britain, France, and Italy, emphasizing the political and administrative constraints involved in all three countries, is contained in Jack Hayward and Michael Watson, eds., *Planning, Politics and Public Policy.*

37. Sundquist, *Dispersing Population*, pp. 183–87.

38. Frances and John Wakeford, "Universities and the Study of Elites," in *Elites and Power in British Society*, ed. Philip Stanworth and Anthony Giddens, pp. 185–97.

39. Harold J. Perkin, *Innovation in the New Universities of the United Kingdom*; Tyrell Burgess and John Pratt, *Technical Education in the United Kingdom.*

40. Perkin, *Innovation*, pp. 1–3.

41. E. Böning and K. Roeloffs, *Three German Universities: Aachen, Bochum, Konstanz.*

42. Ibid., pp. 120–21.

43. See chapter on France in *Academic Power*, ed. John H. Van de Graaff.

44. Sidney Tarrow, "Local Constraints on Regional Reform: A Comparison of Italy and France," pp. 1–36.

CHAPTER FIVE

1. Emile Durkheim, *The Division of Labor in Society*. See particularly his preface to the second edition, "Some Notes on Occupational Groups," pp. 1–31.

2. Hastings Rashdall, *The Universities of Europe in the Middle Ages*, 1:151–54; Sylvia L. Thrupp, "Gilds," in *International Encyclopedia of Social Sciences*, 6:184–87.

3. *Webster's New International Dictionary*, second edition, unabridged (Springfield, Mass.: G. & C. Merriam Co., 1934).

4. French and Italian usage refers to the occupational guilds as

"corporations." Thus, Durkheim wrote of "the corporation or occupational group" in his classic claim for the importance of guild-like organization. See especially the preface to the second edition, "Some Notes on Occupational Groups," in Durkheim, *Division of Labor*, pp. 1–31.

5. See Max Weber, *General Economic History*, p. 148; Thrupp, "Gilds," pp. 184–85; Durkheim, *Division of Labor*, pp. 7–10.

6. Thrupp, "Gilds," p. 185; Durkheim, *Division of Labor*, pp. 12–18.

7. Karl Marx, *Pre-Capitalist Economic Formations*.

8. Weber, *Economic History*, p. 141.

9. Ibid., p. 142.

10. Ibid., p. 138.

11. Ibid., pp. 136–37.

12. Thrupp, "Gilds," pp. 185–87.

13. John W. Baldwin, "Introduction," in *Universities in Politics*, ed. John W. Baldwin and Richard A. Goldthwaite.

14. Ibid., p. 5.

15. Ibid., p. 8.

16. Rashdall, *Universities of Europe*, 1:18.

17. Ibid., 1:19.

18. Marx, *Economic Formations*, pp. 109, 135.

19. Durkheim, *Division of Labor*, passim, and especially the preface to the second edition, pp. 1–31. See also Thrupp, "Gilds," p. 187.

20. Thrupp, "Gilds," p. 187.

21. Arthur L. Stinchcombe, "Social Structure and Organizations," in *Handbook of Organizations*, ed. James G. March, p. 169. See pages 153–69 of this article for an excellent delineation of why organizational forms created in the past often continue and do well in the present, despite their apparent anachronistic nature.

22. Reeves speaks of the development of the guild form of organization from the medieval period "right down to the present age" and comments: "The astonishing thing is that the medieval-guild model has served the Western universities so long and has shaped so powerfully the thinking of so many academic generations," in comparison with "the industrial-plant concept" and other modern models. Marjorie Reeves, "The European University from Medieval Times," in *Higher Education*, ed. W. R. Niblett, p. 64.

23. A general statement for which the United States is the main deviant case. Without medieval origins, American academic organization has been shaped extensively by the conditions under which colonial colleges were founded and the later conditions in the last half of the nineteenth century under which old colleges evolved into universities, and new universities were founded. The early conditions favored control from the top in the form of trustee authority; the later conditions control

from the top in the form of presidential leadership and bureaucratic staff, in addition to trustees. American faculties traditionally were not self-organizing and were easily hired and fired by superiors. Faculty strength evolved later, essentially in the twentieth century, and always within the frameworks established earlier. The model for faculty strength in the late-developing American university was the guild authority of the German professor. See Richard Hofstadter and Walter P. Metzger, *The Development of Academic Freedom in the United States*; Burton R. Clark, "The United States," in *Academic Power*, ed. John H. Van de Graaff.

With the United States primarily in mind, and the British scene secondarily, James S. Coleman has noted that "the university, along with the family, is one of the few social institutions remaining from medieval times, and . . . its structural characteristics reflect its history," causing it now to be a "curious mixture of a modern corporate actor and a medieval community." Coleman, "The University and Society's New Demands Upon It," in *Content and Context*, ed. Carl Kaysen, p. 366, 375.

24. Hence it combines certain items set forth in Weber's broad treatment of authority—rule by notables, patrimonialism, and collegial government—which have been disregarded in the recent emphasis on bureaucracy and charisma. See Guenther Roth, "Personal Rulership, Patrimonialism, and Empire-Building in the New States." pp. 194–206.

25. Eric Ashby, for example, uses the term "guild" broadly in two ways that highlight horizontal connection: as a local body of teachers of whom loyalty is demanded to the local university; and as "a second guild" (the professional guild) of peers in a far-flung discipline. Ashby, *Adapting Universities to a Technological Society*, chap. 6, "The Academic Profession."

26. These reasons for persistence of a form of organization are developed in Stinchcombe, "Social Structure," pp. 167–69.

27. Pier Paolo Giglioli, "The Italian University between Patrimonialism and Bureaucracy."

28. Gaetano Mosca, *The Ruling Class*, p. 481.

29. Talcott Parsons, "Professions," in *International Encyclopedia of the Social Sciences*, 12:545.

30. Matthew Arnold, *Schools and Universities on the Continent*, p. xi.

31. Ibid.

32. Some progress has been made in recent work, principally in Britain and the United States. On Britain, see Graeme C. Moodie and Rowland Eustace, *Power and Authority in British Universities*; Edward Boyle and Anthony Crosland (in conversation with Maurice Kogan), *The Politics of Education*; A. H. Halsey and M. A. Trow, *The British Academics*, chap. 4, "University Autonomy," and chap. 5, "University

Government"; Robert O. Berdahl, *British Universities and the State.* On the United States, see Leon D. Epstein, *Governing the University*; Carlos E. Kruytbosch and Sheldon L. Messinger, eds., *The State of the University*; J. Victor Baldridge, ed., *Academic Governance*; Michael D. Cohen and James G. March, *Leadership and Ambiguity*; James A. Perkins, ed., *The University as an Organization*; Eugene C. Lee and Frank M. Bowen, *The Multicampus University.*

33. Ashby, *Universities: British, Indian, African*; Reeves, "The European University"; Halsey and Trow, *British Academics*; Moodie and Eustace, *British Universities.*

34. Laurence R. Veysey, *The Emergence of the American University.*

35. E. D. Duryea, "Evolution of University Organization," in *University as an Organization*, ed. James A. Perkins, chap. 2, especially pp. 23-31.

BIBLIOGRAPHY

Adams, John Clarke, and Barile, Paolo. *The Government of Republican Italy.* 2d ed. Boston: Houghton Mifflin, 1966.

Ammassari, Paolo; Dell'Orto, Frederica Garzonio; and Ferraresi, Franco, *Il burocrate di fronte alla burocrazia.* Milan: Guiffrè, 1969.

Arnold, Matthew. *Schools and Universities on the Continent.* London: Macmillan, 1868.

Ashby, Eric. *Adapting Universities to a Technological Society.* San Francisco: Jossey-Bass, 1974.

_____. "The Structure of Higher Education: A World View." Occasional Paper No. 6, International Council for Educational Development. New York: 1973.

_____. *Universities: British, Indian, African: A Study in the Ecology of Higher Education.* Cambridge, Mass.: Harvard University Press, 1966.

Bain, Joe S. *International Differences in Industrial Structure: Eight Nations in the 1950s.* New Haven: Yale University Press, 1966.

Baldridge, J. Victor, ed. *Academic Governance.* Berkeley: McCutchan Publishing Corporation, 1971.

Baldwin, John W., and Goldthwaite, Richard A., eds. *Universities in Politics: Case Studies from the Late Middle Ages and Early Modern Period.* Baltimore: The Johns Hopkins University Press, 1972.

Barbagli, Marzio. *Disoccupazione intellettuale e sistema scolastico in Italia.* Bologna: Il Mulino, Universale Paperbacks (UPM 4), 1974.

Ben-David, Joseph. *The Scientist's Role in Society: A Comparative Study.* Englewood Cliffs, N.J.: Prentice-Hall, 1971.

Berdahl, Robert O. *British Universities and the State.* Berkeley: University of California Press, 1959.

Bobbio, Norberto. "Trends in Italian Legal Theory." *American Journal of Comparative Law* 8 (1959):329–40.

Böning, E., and Roeloffs, K. *Three German Universities: Aachen, Bochum, Konstanz.* Paris: Organisation for Economic Co-operation and Development (OECD), 1970.

Boyle, Edward, and Crosland, Anthony. *The Politics of Education.* Middlesex, England: Penguin Books, 1971.

Bruno, Sergio. "Dimensioni economiche di una riforma universitaria." *Economia del lavoro* 2, nos. 2-3 (1971):122-52.

Burgess, Tyrell, and Pratt, John. *Technical Education in the United Kingdom.* Paris: Organisation for Economic Co-operation and Development (OECD), 1971.

Butts, R. Freeman. *The Education of the West.* New York: McGraw-Hill, 1973.

Buzzati-Traverso, Adriano, et al. *L'organizzazione della ricerca scientifica.* Rome: Edizioni della voce, 1968.

Cappelletti, Luciano. "The Italian Bureaucracy: A Study of the *Carriera Direttiva* of the Italian Administration." Ph.D. dissertation, University of California, Berkeley, 1966. Published in Italy as *Burocrazia e società.* Milan: Dott. A. Giuffrè, Editore, 1968.

Cappelletti, Mauro; Merryman, John Henry; and Perillo, Joseph M. *The Italian Legal System.* Stanford: Stanford University Press, 1967.

Caracciolo, Alberto. "Autonomia o centralizzazione degli studi superiori nella età della destra." *Rassegna storica del risorgimento,* 1958, pp. 573-603.

Carr-Saunders, A. M., and Wilson, P. A. *The Professions.* Oxford: Oxford University Press, 1933.

Centro studi investimenti sociali (CENSIS). "I livelli medi di istruzione della popolazione in Italia e negli Stati Uniti." *Quindicinale di Note e Commenti* 2, no. 25 (15 June 1966):13-15.

————. "La partecipazione femminile all'aumento della scolarità dell' obbligo." *Quindicinale di Note e Commenti,* 1, no. 11 (15 November 1965):8-30.

————. "Scuola, famiglia e mobilità sociale." *Quindicinale di Note e Commenti* 2, nos. 19-20 (1 April 1966):20-28.

Cipolla, Carlo M. "The Economic Decline of Italy." In *Crisis and Change in the Venetian Economy,* edited by Brian S. Pullan. London: Methuen, 1968.

Clark, Burton R. "The 'Cooling-Out' Function in Higher Education." *The American Journal of Sociology* 65 (May 1960):569-76.

————. *The Open Door College.* New York: McGraw-Hill, 1960.

Clark, Terry Nichols. *Prophets and Patrons: The French University and The Emergence of the Social Sciences.* Cambridge, Mass.: Harvard University Press, 1973.

Cobban, Alan B. "Medieval Student Power." *Past and Present,* no. 53 (1971), pp. 38-40, 44-45, 61-64.

Cochrane, Eric. *Florence in the Forgotten Centuries: 1527-1800.* Chicago: The University of Chicago Press, 1973.

Cohen, Michael D., and March, James G. *Leadership and Ambiguity: The American College President.* New York: McGraw-Hill, 1974.

Coleman, James S. "The University and Society's New Demands Upon It." In *Content and Context: Essays on College Education,* edited by Carl Kaysen, pp. 359-99. New York: McGraw-Hill, 1973.

Comitato di studio dei problemi dell'Università italiana. *Finanziamento e spese dell'Università.* Studi sull'Università italiana, vol. 4. Bologna: Il Muiino, 1963.

————. *La popolazione universitaria.* Studi sull'Università italiana, vol. 1. Bologna: Il Mulino, 1960.

Coulborn, Ruston, ed. *Feudalism in History.* Hamden, Conn.: Archon Books, 1965.

Crane, Diana. *Invisible Colleges: Diffusion of Knowledge in Scientific Communities.* Chicago: The University of Chicago Press, 1973.

Dalton, Melville. *Men Who Manage.* New York: John Wiley & Sons, 1959.

De Marchi, Franco. *La burocrazia centrale in Italia.* Milan: Guiffrè, 1965.

de Ruggiero, Guido. *The History of European Liberalism.* Boston: Beacon Press, 1959.

de Tocqueville, Alexis. *Democracy in America.* New York: Vintage Books, 1954.

Di Renzo, Gordon J. "Sociology in Italy Today." *International Review of Modern Sociology* 2 (March 1972):1-26.

Driver, Christopher. *The Exploding University.* Indianapolis: Bobbs-Merrill, 1971.

Durkheim, Emile. *The Division of Labor in Society.* Glencoe, Illinois: The Free Press, 1947.

Duryea, E. D. "Evolution of University Organization." In *The University as an Organization,* edited by James A. Perkins, chap. 2. New York: McGraw-Hill, 1973.

Epstein, Leon D. *Governing the University.* San Francisco: Jossey-Bass, 1974.

Etzioni, Amitai. *The Semi-Professions and Their Organization.* New York: The Free Press, 1969.

Ferrarotti, Franco. "Management in Italy." In F. Harbison and C. A. Myers, *Management in the Industrial World.* New York: McGraw-Hill, 1959.

Frank, Andrew. "Goal Ambiguity and Conflicting Standards: An Approach to the Study of Organizations." *Human Organization* 17 (1958):8-13.

Freddi, Giorgio. "Legitimacy and Opposition in the Italian Judiciary: A

Study of Organizational Conflict." Ph.D. dissertation, University of California, Berkeley, 1970.

Freidson, Eliot. *Professional Dominance: The Social Structure of Medical Care.* New York: Atherton Press, 1970.

Fried, Robert C. *The Italian Prefects: A Study in Administrative Politics.* New Haven: Yale University Press, 1963.

Froio, Felice. *Università e classe politica.* Milan: Edizioni di Comunità, 1968.

————. *Università: mafia e potere.* Florence: "La Nuova Italia" Editrice, 1973.

Galli, Giorgio, and Prandi, Alfonso. *Patterns of Political Participation in Italy.* New Haven: Yale University Press, 1970.

Germino, Dante, and Passigli, Stefano. *The Government and Politics of Contemporary Italy.* New York: Harper and Row, 1968.

Giglioli, Pier Paolo. "The Italian University between Patrimonialism and Bureaucracy." Ph.D. dissertation, University of California, Berkeley. Published in Italian as *L'Università italiana tra patrimonialismo e burocrazia.* Bologna: Il Mulino (forthcoming).

Gilpin, Robert. *France in the Age of the Scientific State.* Princeton, N.J.: Princeton University Press, 1968.

Goode, William J. "A Theory of Role Strain." *American Sociological Review* 25 (August 1960):483–96.

Halsey, A. H., and Trow, M. A. *The British Academics.* Cambridge, Mass.: Harvard University Press, 1971.

Harbison, Frederick, and Myers, Charles A. *Education, Manpower and Economic Growth.* New York: McGraw-Hill, 1964.

Haskins, Charles Homer. *The Rise of Universities.* Ithaca, New York: Cornell University Press, 1957.

Hay, Denys. Introduction. In *The New Cambridge Modern History.* Volume 1, *The Renaissance 1493–1520,* planned by G. R. Potter; edited with a new Preface by Denys Hay. Cambridge: Cambridge University Press, 1957. Paperback edition, 1975.

————. "Schools and Universities." In *The New Cambridge Modern History.* Volume 2, *The Reformation 1520–1559,* edited by G. R. Elton. Cambridge: Cambridge University Press, 1958. Paperback edition, 1975.

Hayward, Jack, and Watson, Michael, eds. *Planning, Politics and Public Policy.* Cambridge: Cambridge University Press, 1975.

Heclo, Hugh, and Wildavsky, Aaron. *The Private Government of Public Money.* Berkeley and Los Angeles: University of California Press, 1974.

Hildebrand, George. *Growth and Structure in the Economy of Modern Italy.* Cambridge, Mass.: Harvard University Press, 1965.

Hirschman, Albert O. *Exit, Voice, and Loyalty.* Cambridge: Harvard University Press, 1970.

Hofstadter, Richard, and Metzger, Walter P. *The Development of Academic Freedom in the United States.* New York: Columbia University Press, 1955.

Hughes, H. Stuart. *Consciousness and Society.* New York: Alfred A. Knopf, 1961.

I Deputati e Senatori del Quinto Parlamento Repubblicano. Rome: Casa Editrice "La Navicella," 1968.

International Handbook of Universities: And Other Institutions of Higher Education. 5th ed. Edited by H. M. R. Keyes and D. J. Aitken. Paris: The International Association of Universities, 1971.

Italy, Consiglio nazionale delle ricerche. *Relazione del Presidente del C.N.R. sullo stato della ricerca scientifica e technologica in Italia per il 1973.* Rome: 1974.

Italy, Istituto centrale di statistica. *Annuario statistico dell'istruzione italiana*, vol. 14, 1962. Rome: 1963.

————. *Annuario statistico dell'istruzione italiana*, vol. 19, 1967. Rome: 1968.

————. *Annuario statistico dell'istruzione italiana*, vol. 24, 1972. Rome: 1973.

Italy, Istituto di statistica, Facoltà di scienze statistiche demografiche ed attuariali, Università degli studi di Roma. *Gli assistenti universitari e i liberi docenti in Italia.* Rome: 1969.

Italy, Ministero della pubblica istruzione. *Relazione della commissione di indagine sullo stato e sullo sviluppo della pubblica istruzione in Italia.* Rome: 1963.

————. *Relazione sullo stato della pubblica istruzione in Italia.* Rome: 1963.

Italy, Ministero della pubblica istruzione, Direzione generale dell'istruzione universitaria. *Disposizioni sull'ordinamento didattico universitario.* Rome: Istituto poligrafico dello stato, 1966.

————. *Università e istituti universitari.* Rome: Istituto poligrafico dello stato, 1966.

Italy, *Ruoli di anzianità del personale insegnante delle Università e degli Istituti Superiori d'istruzione.* Rome: Istituto poligrafico dello stato, 1968.

James, Edith E. Coulson. *Bologna: Its History, Antiquities and Art.* London: Oxford University Press, 1909.

Jamous, H., and Peloille, B. "Changes in the French University–Hospital System." In *Professions and Professionalization*, ed. J. A. Jackson, pp. 111–52. Cambridge: Cambridge University Press, 1970.

Johnson, Harry G. "National Styles in Economic Research: The United

States, The United Kingdom, Canada, and Various European Coun-
tries." *Daedalus*, Spring 1973, pp. 65–74.
Jones, P. J. "Communes and Despots: The City State in Late-Medieval
Italy." *Transactions of the Royal Historical Society*, 5th series, vol. 15,
1965, pp. 79–80.
Jorio, Giuseppe. *Legislazione universitaria*. Naples: Libreria scientifica
editrice, 1968.
Kagan, Richard L. *Students and Society in Early Modern Spain*.
Baltimore: The Johns Hopkins University Press, 1974.
Kaufman, Herbert. *The Forest Ranger: A Study in Administrative
Behavior*. Baltimore: The Johns Hopkins University Press, 1960.
_____. *The Limits of Organizational Change*. University, Alabama:
The University of Alabama Press, 1971.
Kogan, Norman. *The Government of Italy*. New York: Thomas Y.
Crowell, 1962.
Kruytbosch, Carlos E., and Messinger, Sheldon L., eds. *The State of the
University: Authority and Change*. Beverly Hills, Calif.: Sage Publica-
tions, 1970.
La Palombara, Joseph. *Interest Groups in Italian Politics*. Princeton:
Princeton University Press, 1964.
Lee, Eugene C., and Bowen, Frank M. *The Multicampus University: A
Study of Academic Governance*. New York: McGraw-Hill, 1971.
Lindblom, Charles E. *The Intelligence of Democracy: Decision Making
Through Mutual Adjustment*. New York: The Free Press, 1965.
_____. "The Science of 'Muddling Through'." *Public Administration
Review* 19 (Spring 1959):79–88.
Lodahl, Janice Beyer, and Gordon, Gerald. "The Structure of Scientific
Fields and the Functioning of University Graduate Departments."
American Sociological Review 37 (February 1972):57–72.
Lutz, Vera. *Italy: A Study in Economic Development*. London: Oxford
University Press, 1962.
McConnell, Grant. *Private Power and American Democracy*. New York:
Alfred A. Knopf, 1966.
Mancini, Federico. "From Reform to Adventure." *Dissent*, no. 72
(Sept.–Oct. 1969), pp. 413–22.
_____. "The Italian Student Movement." *American Association of
University Professors Bulletin* 54 (Winter 1968):427–32.
Martinotti, Guido. "Italy." In *Students, University & Society*, edited by
Margaret Scotford Archer. London: Heinemann Educational Books,
1972.
Marx, Karl. *Pre-Capitalist Economic Formations*. Translated by Jack
Cohen. Introduction by E. J. Hobsbawm, ed. New York: International
Publishers, 1965.

Merton, Robert K. *Social Theory and Social Structure*. Glencoe, Illinois: The Free Press, 1957.

Metzger, Walter. "The Academic Profession and Its Public Critics." In *The Public Challenge and the Campus Response*, edited by Robert A. Altman and Carolyn M. Byerly. Boulder, Colorado: Western Interstate Commission for Higher Education, 1971.

Michels, Robert. *Political Parties: A Sociological Study of the Oligarchical Tendencies of Modern Democracy*. Glencoe, Illinois: The Free Press, 1949.

Moodie, Graeme C., and Eustace, Rowland. *Power and Authority in British Universities*. Montreal: McGill-Queen's University Press, 1974.

Mosca, Gaetano. *The Ruling Class: Elementi di Scienza Politica*. Translated by Hannah D. Kahn. Edited and revised, with an introduction by Arthur Livingston. New York: McGraw-Hill, 1939.

Organisation for Economic Co-operation and Development (OECD). *Development of Higher Education, 1950–1967. Analytical Report.* Paris: 1971.

———. *Development of Higher Education, 1950–1967. Statistical Survey.* Paris: 1970.

———. *Italy*. The Mediterranean Regional Project: Country Reports. Paris: 1965.

———. *Quantitative Trends in Teaching Staff in Higher Education.* Paris: 1971.

———. *Reviews of National Policies For Education: Italy.* Paris: 1969.

———. *Reviews of National Science Policies: Italy.* ("The Brooks Report.") Paris: 1968.

Parsons, Talcott. "Professions." In *International Encyclopedia of the Social Sciences*, vol. 12, pp. 536–47. New York: The Macmillan Company and The Free Press, 1968.

Patterson, Michelle. "Conflict, Power and Structure: The Organization and Reform of the French University." Ph.D. dissertation, Yale University, 1975.

Perkin, Harold J. *Innovation in the New Universities of the United Kingdom*. Paris: Organisation for Economic Co-operation and Development (OECD), 1968.

Perkins, James A., ed. *The University as an Organization*. New York: McGraw-Hill, 1973.

Pressman, Jeffrey L., and Wildavsky, Aaron B. *Implementation*. Berkeley: University of California Press, 1973.

Putnam, Robert D., *The Beliefs of Politicians: Ideology, Conflict, and Democracy in Britain and Italy*. New Haven: Yale University Press, 1973.

Rashdall, Hastings. *The Universities of Europe in the Middle Ages*. A new edition in three volumes, edited by F. M. Powicke and A. B. Emden. (First edition, 1895.) Oxford: Oxford University Press, 1936.

Reeves, Marjorie. "The European University from Medieval Times." In *Higher Education: Demand & Response*, edited by W. R. Niblett, pp. 61-84. San Francisco: Jossey-Bass, 1970.

Roth, Guenther. "Personal Rulership, Patrimonialism, and Empire-Building in the New States." *World Politics* 20 (1968):194-206.

Sandulli, Aldo M. *Codice della legislazione amministrativa*. 2 vols. Rome: Casa editrice stamperia nazionale, 1965.

Sanna, Emilio. "I cervelli en esilio." *Tempo* 31, no. 10 (March 8, 1969): 20-26.

Schachner, Nathan. *The Medieval Universities*. New York: Frederick A. Stokes, 1938.

Seiber, Sam D. "Toward a Theory of Role Accumulation." *American Sociological Review* 39 (August 1974):567-78.

Seidman, Harold. *Politics, Position & Power: The Dynamics of Federal Organization*. New York: Oxford University Press, 1970.

Selznick, Philip. "The Sociology of Law." In *International Encyclopedia of the Social Sciences*, vol. 9, pp. 50-59. New York: The Macmillan Company and The Free Press, 1968.

Seton-Watson, Christopher. *Italy from Liberalism to Fascism: 1870-1925*. London: Methuen, 1967.

Simonini, R. C., Jr. *The Universities of Italy*. Rome: The American Commission for Cultural Exchange with Italy, 1961.

Smith, Denis Mack. *Italy: A Modern History*. Ann Arbor: The University of Michigan Press, 1959.

Snoek, J. Diedrick. "Role Strain in Diversified Role Sets." *American Journal of Sociology* 71 (1966):363-72.

Sprigge, Cecil. *Benedetto Croce*. New Haven: Yale University Press, 1952.

Statera, Gianni. *Death of a Utopia: The Development and Decline of Student Movements in Europe*. New York: Oxford University Press, 1975.

Stinchcombe, Arthur L. "Social Structure and Organizations." In *Handbook of Organizations*, edited by James G. March. Chicago: Rand McNally, 1965.

Suleiman, Ezra N. *Politics, Power, and Bureaucracy in France: The Administrative Elite*. Princeton, N.J.: Princeton University Press, 1974.

Sundquist, James L. *Dispersing Population: What America Can Learn from Europe*. Washington, D.C.: The Brookings Institution, 1975.

Tannenbaum, Arnold S.; Kavcic, Bogdan; Rosner, Manachem; Vianello, Mino; and Wieser, Georg. *Hierarchy in Organizations*. San Francisco: Jossey-Bass, 1974.

Tarrow, Sidney. "Local Constraints on Regional Reform: A Comparison of Italy and France." *Comparative Politics* 7 (October 1974):1–36.

Thayer, John A. *Italy and the Great War: Politics and Culture, 1870-1915*. Madison: The University of Wisconsin Press, 1964.

Thrupp, Sylvia L. "Gilds." In *International Encyclopedia of the Social Sciences*, vol. 6, pp. 184–87. New York: The Macmillan Company and The Free Press, 1968.

_____. "The Gilds." In *Economic Organization and Policies in the Middle Ages*, edited by M. M. Postan, E. E. Rich, and Edward Miller. *The Cambridge Economic History of Europe*, vol. 3. Cambridge: At the University Press, 1963.

Van de Graaff, John H., ed. *Academic Power: Patterns of Authority in Seven National Systems of Higher Education* (forthcoming).

_____. "The Politics of German University Reform, 1810-1970." Ph.D. dissertation, Columbia University, 1972.

Veysey, Laurence R. *The Emergence of the American University*. Chicago: University of Chicago Press, 1965.

Wakeford, Frances and John. "Universities and the Study of Elites." In *Elites and Power in British Society*, edited by Philip Stanworth and Anthony Giddens, pp. 185–97. Cambridge: Cambridge University Press, 1974.

Waley, Daniel. *The Italian City-Republics*. New York: McGraw-Hill, 1969.

Warren, Roland L. "The Interorganizational Field as a Focus for Investigation." *Administrative Science Quarterly* 12 (December 1967): 396–419.

Weber, Max. *General Economic History*. Glencoe, Illinois: The Free Press, 1950.

Max Weber: The Theory of Social and Economic Organization. Translated by A. M. Henderson and Talcott Parsons. New York: Oxford University Press, 1947.

Willis, F. Roy. *Italy Chooses Europe*. New York: Oxford University Press, 1971.

Wilson, Woodrow. *Congressional Government*. New York: Meridian Books, 1956.

INDEX

Academic Senate (*Senato Accademico*), in Italian universities, 69, 89
Adams, John Clarke, 179 nn. 24, 30; 183 n. 41; 184 n. 43
Administration, University. *See* Bureaucracy, in Italian higher education
Administrative Council (*Consiglio di Amministrazione*), in Italian universities, 89
Administrative director (*Direttore Amministrativo*), in Italian universities, 66-67, 145
Admission, university, in Italy, 20-22, 48, 118-19
American higher education; academic guilds in, 170-72; reforms of, 150; selection of personnel, 61
Arnold, Mathew, 14, 47, 166, 176 n. 26; 179 n. 37; 189 nn. 30-31
Ashby, Eric, 185 nn. 1, 5; 187 n. 7; 189 n. 25; 190 n. 33

Bain, Joe S., 185 n. 2
Baldridge, J. Victor, 190 n. 32
Baldwin, John W., 175 n. 3; 188 nn. 13, 14, 15
Balkanization: in American public administration, 42; in Italian

higher education, 67-74, 145, 162; in Italian public administration, 41-43
Barbagli, Marzio, 178 n. 15; 180 nn. 44, 46
Barile, Paolo, 179 nn. 24, 30; 183 n. 41
Ben-David, Joseph, 15; 176 nn. 28, 29, 30, 31
Bo, Carlo, 89
Bobbio, Norberto, 179 n. 30
Böning, E., 187 nn. 41, 42
Bowen, Frank M., 190 n. 32
British higher education: academic guilds in, 169-70; reform in, 150-51; selection of personnel, 61; structure of, 46
Bruno, Sergio, 179 n. 38; 180 n. 48
Bureaucracy, in Italian higher education, 45-74; balkanization, 67-74; levels of organization, 46-47; limits of control, 73-74; means of control, 65-67; nationalized sectors of decision-making, 47-65; particularism within, 106-13; penetrated by guild control, 161-73
Bureaucracy, in Italian public administration, 35-45; administrative culture, 43-45; balkanization, 41-43; centralization